THE LOUISIANA MAYOR'S COURT

An Overview and Its Constitutional Problems

FLOYD A. BURAS, III

authorHOUSE®

AuthorHouse™
1663 Liberty Drive
Bloomington, IN 47403
www.authorhouse.com
Phone: 1 (800) 839-8640

Published by AuthorHouse 12/23/2015

ISBN: 978-1-5049-7033-4 (sc)
ISBN: 978-1-5049-7032-7 (e)

Library of Congress Control Number: 2015921276

Print information available on the last page.

INTRODUCTION

Mayor's courts in Louisiana pose two threats to the right of procedural due process guaranteed under the constitution. The first threat is that defendants before these courts do not receive a fair trial by a neutral decision maker. This is because the mayor, who presides over court, has an inherent pecuniary interest to find defendants guilty so as to assess fines and raise general fund revenue for the city.[1] Secondly, the potential for the mayor's financial bias is compounded by the fact that mayor's courts operate with virtually little to no rules of procedure or oversight.[2] This enables to mayor to administer court and render arbitrary decisions with relatively unbridled discretion, which also creates a lack of procedural uniformity in these courts across the state.

The mayor's court is the most numerous type of court in Louisiana with over 250 of these courts across the state.[3] Under this scheme the mayor essentially serves as prosecutor and judge to determine guilt for violations of certain municipal ordinances.[4] Though the mayor is not required to have a law license or any form of legal training, he is empowered to determine guilt and assess penalties with little oversight and very few formal rules.[5] He may impose fines and/or imprisonment, and also suspend the execution of imposed sentences in whole or in part and place defendants on unsupervised

---

[1] *Infra.*

[2] *Infra.*

[3] Supreme Court of Louisiana, Annual Report 2013 of the Judicial Council of the Supreme Court 19-20 (2013).

[4] La. Rev. Stat. § 33:441.

[5] *Infra.*

or supervised probation.[6] The mayor may adjudicate municipal ordinances that are civil in nature such as zoning violations and speed camera tickets, and criminal or quasi-criminal in nature such as misdemeanor violations and traffic tickets.[7]

The first constitutional problem presented in this article is that mayors have a financial incentive to find defendants guilty so that fines can be assessed and collected. In cities that have mayor's courts the mayor has two roles, the first as the chief executive of the municipality, and second is a judicial role as the presiding officer over the mayor's court.[8] Under his executive role the mayor has the duty to raise general fund revenue for the city. The responsibility for generating income is inherent to the position of mayor and can not be separated.[9] However, mayors are supposed to separate themselves from this when acting in their judicial role so that they do not cast predetermined judgments just to raise revenue by collecting fines.

The U.S. Supreme Court has held that it is reasonable to question the neutrality of a mayor presiding over court.[10] This is because the inherent duty to produce more revenue from fines creates a "possible temptation" that would cause an average mayor to decide cases more favorably against defendants.[11] This is especially true when the town receives a substantial portion of its income from the collection of fines, which courts have found the threshold to be as little as 10% of general fund revenue.[12] Despite the U.S. Supreme Court's rulings, each year mayors through these courts collect millions of dollars in fines, with over 100 cities getting a substantial portion of its general fund revenue from fines.[13] Table 1 (see appendix) provides a list of 100 cities with mayor's courts that collected a substantial portion of

---

[6] La. Rev. Stat. § 33:441.A.(2).

[7] *Infra.*

[8] *Infra.*

[9] *Infra.*

[10] *Infra.*

[11] *Infra.*

[12] *Infra.*

[13] *See* Table 1.

its general fund revenue from fines during their 2013 fiscal year.[14] As Table 1 shows many cities collect significant amounts of money through fine revenue, with cities such as Georgetown raising 94% of its general fund revenue from fines, and Gretna collecting over $5.3 million dollars in fine revenue.

As the second constitutional problem presented will show, mayors are able to administer court with very little statutory guidance. Primarily, mayor's courts operate without any formal rules of procedure because neither the Code of Civil Procedure, the Code of Criminal Procedure, nor the Code of Evidence is applicable to them.[15] It can be implied that the legislature intended for these proceedings to be informal since mayor's courts are excluded from formal codified procedural rules.[16] However, this lack of procedural rules allows the opportunity for mayors to arbitrarily conduct court, collect and use evidence against an accused, and circumvent discovery rules in unfair ways that can deprive defendants of their liberty and property.[17] The codes of procedure were created to help safeguard due process by allowing all courts on the same level to operate similar to one another.[18] But, the lack of formal rules allows each of the 250 mayor's courts to operate in a non-uniform manner which can weaken the integrity of the judicial system.

This article sheds light on both of these Due Process problems created by mayor's courts in Louisiana. This will be done in three parts. Part one provides a brief overview of the mayor's courts including the authority for their establishment and the need to distinguish these courts from other courts. Part two discusses the *de jure* rules on the books that govern these courts and provide mayors with judicial power to decide guilt and issue penalties. Part three

---

[14] Data was gathered from Louisiana Auditor Reports, which only report fine and forfeiture amounts collected by the municipality, and does not specify whether fines derived from mayor's courts or other sources.

[15] *Infra.*

[16] *Infra.*

[17] *Infra.*

[18] *Infra.*

details the two constitutional problems presented in this article: the first problem being how the dual executive and judicial roles that mayors have has the potential to affect his ability to render a fair and impartial decision; and the second problem being the due process concerns that arise by these courts operating without any formal rules of procedure. Proposed solutions are also given in this part.

PART I

Overview

This part provides a brief overview of mayor's courts through three sections. Section "A" provides some background and historical information of these courts. Section "B" identifies the authority for the existence of these courts in Louisiana today. Lastly, section "C" details the importance of distinguishing these courts from other courts of limited jurisdiction.

A. BACKGROUND

It is unknown for how long the constitutional problems presented in this article have existed because there is very little written about early mayor's courts, including when these courts were first established in Louisiana or why we still have them. It is also unknown if early mayor's courts always contributed substantial amounts of income to the town's general fund revenue. Yet, what we do know is that throughout Louisiana there are about 250 mayor's courts in operation today.[19] In comparison there are only 49 city courts, 3 parish courts, and 43 district courts statewide.[20] Moreover, out of all fifty states, only Louisiana and Ohio still have mayor's courts.[21]

---

[19] Supreme Court of Louisiana, Annual Report 2013 of the Judicial Council of the Supreme Court 19-20 (2013).

[20] *Id.*

[21] National Center for State Courts, State Court Structure Charts (2010), *available at* http://www.courtstatistics.org/Other-Pages/State_Court_Structure_Charts. aspx.

However, several states at some point in the past had mayor's courts but do not anymore.[22]

The history of the mayor's court stems back to England, where it is the most ancient court of the kingdom originally called "The Court of our Sovereign Lady the Queen, Holden before the Mayor and Aldermen of the City of London."[23] There the mayor had authority to preside over this court as he was the chief magistrate of the city of London.[24] This court historically had exclusive jurisdiction over causes that arose within the city limits, and modern jurisdiction was set forth in The Mayor's Court of London Procedure Act 1857.[25] Hence, although Louisiana prides itself in the French civilian law tradition, mayor's courts in Louisiana are rooted from the English common law system.

It's difficult to determine when or how the first mayor's court was established in Louisiana because there is limited information easily accessible about this court. Although not written anywhere, a connection can be inferred to Edward Livingston who was an

---

[22] Examples of cases from state courts that reference the existence of mayor's courts within that state include: *Withers v. State*, 36 Ala. 252 (1860); [4] *Williams v. State*, 63 Ark. 307 (1896); *Bates v. Porter*, 74 Cal. 224 (1887); *Gray v. State*, 2 Del. 76 (1836); *State ex rel. Duke v. Wills*, 49 Fla. 380 (1905); *W. & A. R. Co. v. Atlanta*, 113 Ga. 537 (1901); *Finch v. Marvin*, 46 Iowa 384 (1877); *Bryan v. Bates*, 15 Ill. 87 (1853); *Waldo v. Wallace*, 12 Ind. 479 (1859); *Prell v. McDonald*, 7 Kan. 426 (1871); *Shinkle v. Covington*, 83 Ky. 420 (1885); *Welles v. City of Detroit*, 2 Doug. 77 (Mich. 1845); *Dulany on behalf of Lord Proprietary v. Jenings*, 1 H. & McH. 92 (Md. 1738); *Leonard v. Sparks*, 63 Mo. App. 585 (1890); *Griffin v. State*, 127 Miss. 315 (1921); *Scott v. Fishblate*, 117 N.C. 265 (1895); *State v. Gratz*, 86 N.J.L. 483 (1914); *Simson v. Hart*, 14 Johns. 63 (N.Y. 1816); *Baker v. Marcum & Toomer*, 22 Okla. 21 (1908); *Commonwealth ex rel. Attorney-Gen. v. Conyngham*, 65 Pa. 76 (1870); *Greenville v. Spencer*, 77 S.C. 50 (1907); *Newbern v. McCann*, 105 Tenn. 159 (1900); *Ex parte Scwartz*, 2 Tex. Ct. App. 74 (1877); *Young v. Cannon*, 2 Utah 560 (1880); *Brooks v. Potomac*, 149 Va. 427 (1928); *Rowlesburg v. Zelano*, 74 W. Va. 142 (1914).

[23] Ernest A. Jelf, *London Institutions of Public Importance In Their Legal Aspects*, The Law Times: The Journal and Record of The Law and The lawyers, Volumes 105-106, June 4, 1898, at 101-02.

[24] *Id.*

[25] *Id.*

influential figure in early Louisiana government and also assisted in drafting its first criminal code. Prior to coming to Louisiana, Livingston was the mayor of New York City and in that capacity also served as judge over the New York Mayor's Court.[26] Shortly after the Territory of Orleans was established in 1804, Livingston moved to New Orleans and was commissioned to help establish judicial laws for the new territory.[27] In doing so, he drafted a set of rules for the newly created territorial courts based on the rules he issued in the New York Mayor's Court.[28] One of the newly created courts was the Court of Common Pleas[29], which was a court for minor civil matters, and has been referred to as New Orleans' version of the New York Mayor's Court on which Livingston served.[30]

Nevertheless, there are only a handful of early cases from the Supreme Court of Louisiana (herein referred to as Supreme Court) that mention the mayor's courts. However, these early cases never directly address the constitutional problems presented in this article. For example, in an 1849 case the Supreme Court stated that it lacked jurisdiction to decide the constitutionality of a Legislative Act giving judicial power to mayors, after an appeal was brought challenging a judgment by a mayor rendered for a violation of an ordinance.[31] Additionally, the Supreme Court commented in a 1854 case that prior to the adoption of the Louisiana Constitution of 1845, the legislature under former Acts had granted judicial powers, "and this power [was] so long previously exercised by the Mayor... under these Acts."[32] In

---

[26] Mark F. Fernandez, *New Orleans, A Tale of Two Cities: The Legal System That Wasn't*, Louisiana History: The Journal of the Louisiana Historical Association, Vol. 51, No. 4 (Fall 2010), 389, 399-401.

[27] *Id.*

[28] *Id.*

[29] The Breckinridge Act of 1804 created three courts: the Court of Common Pleas, a Governor's Court, and the Superior Court for the Territory of Orleans.

[30] Mark Fernandez, *Edward Livingston, America, and France: Making Law, in* Empires of the Imagination: Transatlantic Histories of the Louisiana Purchase 258, 276 (Peter J. Kastor & Francois Weil eds. 2009).

[31] *City of Donaldsonville v. Richard*, 4 La. Ann. 83 (1849).

[32] *Lafon v. Dufrocq*, 9 La. Ann. 350, 351 (1854).

similar fashion, the Supreme Court in 1858 held that "the Mayor..., under the Act of 1832, had the power to issue the warrant for the arrest of the plaintiff".[33]

B. AUTHORITY FOR THEIR EXISTENCE TODAY

Despite the lack of historical knowledge on the original establishment of Louisiana mayor's courts, today authority for them is provided pursuant to the Louisiana Constitution of 1974 (hereby referred to as Constitution). La. Const. art. V, § 1 states: "The judicial power is vested in a supreme court, courts of appeal, district courts and *other courts* authorized by this Article" (Emphasis added).[34] Mayor's courts are included within such "other courts" by virtue of La. Const. art. V, § 20.[35] This provision provides for the continuation of mayor's courts which predated the 1974 Constitution as follows: "Mayors' courts... existing on the effective date of this constitution are continued, subject to change by law." The drafters' intent of La. Const. art. V, § 20 was "to continue... mayors' courts, subject to the power of the Legislature to regulate, restructure, maintain or abolish such offices."[36]   Yet, because their existence is vested in the constitution, the only way to completely abolish use of these courts is through a constitutional amendment approved by a majority vote of the people.[37]

Consequently, after 1974 municipalities may not establish their own mayor's court by municipal ordinance, because the Constitution vested the power to create courts in the legislature.[38] The goal of this constitutional provision, as stated by Justice Dennis, Chairman of the Drafting Committee for this provision in the Constitutional Convention, was to "provide a vehicle for the legislature if it so

---

[33] *Maguire v. Hughes*, 13 La. Ann. 281 (1858).

[34] La. Const. art. V, § 1.

[35] La. Const. art. V, § 20.

[36] *In re Cedotal*, 97-1291 (La. 2/6/98), 706 So. 2d 1387, 1388.

[37] La. Const. art. XIII, § 1(A)(1).

[38] *Medlen v. State*, 418 So. 2d 618, 622 (La. 1982).

desires over the next period of years to move toward either a three level or four leveled court system that would be uniform and consistent throughout the state and would not be fragmented and specialized as it is today... Because even today, most of our city and other limited jurisdiction courts are really not constitutional courts... Most of them are created by statute pursuant to a grant of authority in this constitution."[39]

Note that La. Const. art. V, § 15 allows the legislature to only establish trial courts of limited jurisdiction with *"parish-wide territorial jurisdiction* and subject matter jurisdiction which shall be uniform throughout the state."[40] However, mayor's courts escape this limitation because they are classified as "tribunals" rather than trial courts.[41] Thus, new mayor's courts may still be created today, but only through the state legislature.

C. THE IMPORTANCE OF IDENTIFYING THE COURT'S CLASSIFICATION

Not all rules are uniform for every type of court of limited jurisdiction. Different rules apply depending on the how the court is classified in the law books (i.e. mayor's court, city court, parish court). Additionally, there are two different categories of mayor's courts, each having different rules that govern them.[42] Distinguishing these classifications is important to understanding which laws apply or don't apply to mayor's courts and why. This section will first illustrate the importance of distinguishing mayor's courts from other courts, and also the confusion the law creates by using improper

---

[39] La. Att'y Gen. Op. No. 1996-0141. However, the legislature enacted subsequent special legislation creating new courts in various cities, including: Village of Forrest in 1999. *See* La. Rev. Stat. § 33:447; Heflin in 2003. *See* La. Rev. Stat. § 33:449; St. Gabriel in 2004. *See* La. Rev. Stat. § 33:450; Clarks in 2006. *See* La. Rev. Stat. § 33:451; Central in 2008. *See* La. Rev. Stat. § 33:453; Ida in 2009. *See* La. Rev. Stat. § 33:441.32; and Hosston in 2010, *See* La. Rev. Stat. § 33:454.

[40] La. Const. art. V, § 15.

[41] *See* La. Code Crim. Proc. art. 931 comment (a).

[42] *Infra.*

terms to identify the types of courts in laws. Secondly, this section identifies the two categories of mayor's courts, and the significance for distinguishing them.

1. THE NEED TO DISTINGUISH MAYOR'S COURTS FROM OTHER COURTS AND THE SEMANTICS PROBLEM

The term "mayor's court" must be distinguished from other courts such as city courts, parish courts, justice of the peace courts, and district courts. Distinguishing these courts is important because Louisiana law provides different rules for each type of these courts.[43] Similarly, procedural rules such as the codes of criminal and civil procedure do not apply to the mayor's courts, but do apply to the other courts of limited jurisdiction.[44] Improper interpretation of these terms may lead some courts to apply inapplicable laws such as the codes of procedure to proceedings in mayor's courts when those rules were not meant to apply.

It should first be noted that there is a distinction between "city courts" and mayor's courts. City courts perform generally the same function of mayor's courts. It's unclear whether a municipality may have both a mayor's court and a city court because there are no laws limiting mayor's courts or requiring their abolishment when a city court is created. Moreover, one of the factors for whether a municipality has to have a city court depends on the population of the ward that the court serves.[45] If a ward contains cities of more

---

[43] Laws defining other courts of limited jurisdiction can be found as follows: City Courts – La. Rev. Stat. § 13:1870 *et seq.*, La. Code Civ. Proc. art. 4901 *et seq.*, La. Code Civ. Proc. art. 5001 *et seq.* (Appeals taken by court of appeal); Parish Courts – La. Rev. Stat. § 13:1455 (Uniform Parish Court Jurisdiction and Procedure Act), La. Code Civ. Proc. art. 4901 *et seq.*, La. Code Civ. Proc. art. 5001 *et seq.* (Appeals taken by court of appeal); Justice of the Peace Courts – La. Rev. Stat. § 13:2586 *et seq.*, La. Code Civ. Proc. art. 4911 *et seq.* (civil jurisdiction).
[44] *Infra* at Part "III.B".
[45] "Except as provided in Chapter 7 of Title 13 of the Louisiana Revised Statutes..., there shall be a mayor's court in the municipality." La. Rev. Stat. § 33:441A(1) (A.(1). City courts are provided for in Chapter 7 of Title 13 of the Revised Statutes.

than five thousand inhabitants then a city court judge must be elected unless specific legislation is provides otherwise.[46] Thus, mayor's courts generally only exist in municipalities with less than 5,000 residents. An additional thing to note is that mayor's courts should not be compared to the municipal or traffic courts in New Orleans. This is because the courts of limited jurisdiction in New Orleans operate under specially enacted legislation.[47]

Mayor's courts can be differentiated from these other courts of limited jurisdiction in two other ways. First, the adjudicator that presides over mayor's courts must either be the mayor or an attorney appointed by the mayor.[48] The other courts of limited jurisdiction are presided over by a "judge" that is elected to that position.[49] Second, Mayor's courts only have jurisdiction to hear violations that occur with the territorial limits of the city for breaches of municipal ordinances.[50]

One problem with identifying whether a particular law applies to mayor's courts is that the laws themselves use ambiguous language to describe the different courts of limited jurisdiction. For example, the Revised Statutes uses the term "municipal court" to describe both mayor's courts and city courts. Notwithstanding, this term seems to be improperly used because it's unclear which types of courts are meant to be included in the term municipal courts.

This is because the laws governing mayor's courts are located in Title 33, Chapter 2... Subpart G entitled "Municipal Courts."[51] The provisions in this subpart pertain only to mayor's courts, and not other types of courts. Moreover, the language of this subpart is preceded by the exclusionary clause: "Except as provided in Chapter

---

[46] La. Rev. Stat. § 13:1872.
[47] *See* La. Rev. Stat. § 13:2491 *et seq.* (Municipal and traffic court of New Orleans); *See* La. Rev. Stat. § 13:2151 *et seq.* (New Orleans City Courts).
[48] La. Rev. Stat. § 33:441.
[49] *See* La. Const. art. V, § 22.
[50] La. Rev. Stat. § 33:441.
[51] La. Rev. Stat. § 33:441 *et seq.*

7 of Title 13 of the Louisiana Revised Statutes...."[52] Chapter 7 is titled "City Courts" and its provisions apply entirely to city courts (with one exception in La. Rev. Stat. § 13:1896).[53] Part I of Chapter 7 is titled "City and Municipal Courts." The scope of Part I is laid out in La. Rev. Stat. § 13:1871 which states in pertinent part "[f]or the purposes of this Part, the term 'city court' includes 'municipal court.'"[54]

Part I of Chapter 7 contains La. Rev. Stat. § 13:1896 which provides the procedures for appealing criminal cases from mayor's courts. However, within this statute there is a distinction between mayor's courts and city, parish, and municipal courts. Paragraph A of this statute provides the procedure for appeals from "mayor's courts," while paragraph B provides a totally different procedure for appeals from "city, parish and municipal courts."[55] Because the term "mayor's courts" in paragraph A is distinguished from the term "municipal courts" in paragraph B, this leaves open the question whether the term "mayor's courts" are meant to be included under the term "municipal court" in Title 13.

Another problem that further obscures proper interpretation is that many municipalities improperly address their mayor's court by the wrong term or use multiple terms interchangeably. For instance, the city of Gretna operates a mayor's court, however the terms "mayor's court," "municipal court," and "city court" are all used randomly to describe its court in the city's Code of Ordinances.[56] Some examples from the City of Gretna Code of Ordinances that illustrate this are as follows: Sec. 18-2(d) "shall compel appearance before the *mayor's court*"; Sec. 15-12 "it shall be the duty of the city to prosecute... violations of this chapter in the *municipal court*";

---

[52] La. Rev. Stat. § 33:441(A)(1). Title 13 contains laws related to Courts and Judicial Procedure.

[53] La. Rev. Stat. § 13:1870.

[54] La. Rev. Stat. § 13:1871.

[55] La. Rev. Stat. § 13:1896.

[56] City of Gretna Code of Ordinances § 18-2(d); § 15-12; § 42-301(c). *See* also La. Rev. Stat. § 33:441.20. (Identifies Gretna's court as a mayor's court).

Sec. 42-301(c) "the city court may issue a summons for the owner to appear in *city court*"). Similarly, another example of this problem can be found with the city of Kenner, which operates a mayor's court.[57] In its Code of Ordinances both the terms "mayor's court," "municipal court" and "city court" are also irregularly used to describe the court throughout various ordinances.[58]

A result of use of the wrong term is that many people and courts may be led into mistakenly believing that certain laws apply to mayor's courts when in actuality they don't. Similarly, since the codes of procedure apply to city courts (but not to mayor's courts), some may improperly apply these rules to mayor's courts as a result of misinterpreting the nomenclature. Thus, proper use and distinction between the types of courts and the terms identifying them should be considered when evaluating whether a law pertains to mayor's courts.

2. TWO CATEGORIES OF MAYOR'S COURTS AND THE LAWS RELATING TO THEM

One of the constitutional problems that this article addresses is the lack of formal rules that control mayor's courts. The majority of the few rules that exist are contained in La. Revised Statutes Title 33 "Municipalities and Parishes". However, the rules provided in La. Rev. Stat. § 33 only apply to municipalities that are incorporated through what is known as a "Lawrason Act" charter.[59] Mayor's courts in town that were not incorporated under the Lawrason Act are not restricted by La. Rev. Stat. § 33 and as a result may conceivably impose harsher penalties for convictions.[60]

---

[57] *See* La. Rev. Stat. § 33:441.1. (Identifies Kenner's court as a mayor's court).

[58] City of Kenner Code of Ordinances: § 16-24(A) "prosecutions shall be before the *mayor's court*"; § 15-2 "required for his appearance in *municipal court*"; § 10-134(a) "A person who violates any of the provision of the article shall be subject to a citation and civil fine... upon proper adjudication before the *Kenner City Court*."

[59] *Infra*.

[60] *Infra*.

The types of charters by which Louisiana municipalities[61] can govern themselves can be divided into two different schemes: (1) "Lawrason Act" or (2) "Non-Lawrason Act" charters. Only about 75% of incorporated political subdivisions use the Lawrason Act framework.[62] Whether the provisions in Title 33 apply to a particular mayor's court depends on the type of charter the municipality was incorporated under. As a result, there are no statewide uniform rules since mayor's courts located in the non-Lawrason Act cities have different rules governing their operation.

The Lawrason Act (La. Rev. Stat. § 33:321 *et seq.*) provides for a traditional form of government, the mayor-board of alderman form, which remains the most common form in the state.[63] Through the Lawrason Act the state legislature supplies a uniform general legislative charter for all municipalities created after 1898 when the Act was passed, and also for prior incorporated municipalities that subsequently elected to adopt the Act through their own initiative.[64] Under La. Rev. Stat. § 33:321, all Lawrason Act municipalities *shall* be governed by the provisions of this Act *except* Non-Lawrason municipalities.[65]

Non-Lawrason municipalities are those governed by either by a special legislative charter, home rule charter, or plan of government adopted pursuant to Article VI of the Constitution. Mayor's courts in these political subdivisions are governed by the charter under which its municipality incorporated. Similarly, courts in these municipalities are not subject to the provisions of the Lawrason Act, unless the municipality elects to adopt the language of the Lawrason Act.[66] However, for municipalities governed by a special legislative charter,

---

[61] "Municipality" is defined as an incorporated city, town, or village. La. Const. art. VI, § 44(3)

[62] Jerry J. Guillot, *The Lawrason Act* 1 (ed. 2008).

[63] La. Rev. Stat. § 33:321 *et seq.*

[64] Jerry J. Guillot, *The Lawrason Act* 1 (ed. 2008).

[65] La. Rev. Stat. § 33:321.

[66] La. Const. art. VI, § 4; La. Const. art. VI, § 6; *See* La. Att'y Gen. Op. No. 2004-0282.

if its charter is silent on a particular matter, then the provisions of the Lawrason Act shall govern.[67] Nevertheless, if a conflict exists between the provisions of the special legislative charter and the Lawrason Act, then the provisions of the special legislative charter shall govern.[68]

The intended purpose of the Lawrason Act is to provide a uniform type of government for municipalities and the mayor's courts.[69] So in theory, the method of operation for mayor's courts in the 75% of municipalities incorporated under the Lawrason Act should be fairly consistent. However, the method of government for the 25% of municipalities not governed by the Lawrason Act may differ from Lawrason and also from other Non-Lawrason municipalities. Thereby leading to the possibility that subject matter jurisdiction (as well as other aspects such as procedure) could be inconsistently established amongst the mayor's courts, depending on how their charters are written.[70]

There are differences in how these two types of entities derive their police powers from the state, and these differences determine what types of penalties can be assessed by mayor's courts. Lawrason

---

[67] La. Rev. Stat. § 33:481.

[68] La. Rev. Stat. § 33:481. An entity created by a special legislative charter is usually one created to perform one major function (i.e. police, water, or fire protection).

A home rule charter allows a municipality to operate under a level of local autonomy from the control of the state. The citizens of such political subdivision select their own form of government and decide how powers and duties will be distributed. The state legislature is constitutionally prohibited from enacting any law which changes or affects the structure and organization or the particular distribution and redistribution of the powers and functions of the local government. Const. Art. VI, §6. Also, the Constitution authorizes any municipality to draft, adopt, and amend a home rule charter. *See* Const. Art. VI, §4.

[69] Jerry J. Guillot, *The Lawrason Act* 1 (ed. 2008).

[70] A noticeable number of court opinions and Attorney General Opinions apparently failed to either recognize or point out this distinction. As a result, much of the jurisprudence discusses aspects of mayor's courts as though they all are governed under the Lawrason Act. However, La. Const. art. VI and La. Rev. Stat. Ann. § 33:421 clearly establish an exception for Non-Lawrason courts.

municipalities derive their police powers through La. Rev. Stat. §
33:361, La. Rev. Stat. § 33:362, and La. Const. art. VI, § 7(A). These
political subdivisions may exercise their police power by enacting
ordinances and provide for their enforcement "by fine not to exceed
five hundred dollars or imprisonment not exceeding sixty days, or
both."[71] Whereas, Non-Lawrason municipality powers are granted
and limited under La. Const. art VI. For example, Home Rule
municipalities possess powers within their jurisdiction that are as
broad as that of the state.[72] Hence, in terms of how harsh penalties
can be for ordinances of Non-Lawrason entities, they are only limited
by the constitution, laws permitted by the constitution, or their own
charter.

As a result, it is conceivable that non-Lawrason municipalities
could be harsher than Lawrason municipalities. For example, the
length of time a Lawrason mayor may sentence a defendant to
imprisonment is limited by statute to sixty days. But non- Lawrason
entities on the other hand are only subject to constitutional limitations,
which could impose sentences of imprisonment up to as much as six
months.[73]

However, neither type of municipality may enact an ordinance
that is defined and provides for the punishment of a felony, or that
governs private or civil relationships, or that abridges the police
power of the state.[74] Additionally, all delegated police powers are
excised concurrently with the state.[75] Thus, mayor's courts only have

---

[71] La. Rev. Stat. Ann. § 33:362A.(2)(b); The board of alderman may also adopt a
schedule of fines for violations of ordinances as part of its police powers to enact
ordinances granted under La. Rev. Stat. § 33:401.

[72] *New Orleans Campaign for a Living Wage v. City of New Orleans*, 2002-0991
(La. 9/4/02), 825 So. 2d 1098, 1103.

[73] See *Duncan v. Louisiana*, 391 U.S. 145, 159 (1968); *See* La. Const. art. I, § 17(A).
Noting that imprisonment over six months requires a jury trial, which is not an
option in mayor's courts.

[74] La. Const. art. VI, § 9; La. Rev. Stat. Ann. § 14:143; *see* generally *City of Baton
Rouge v. Ross*, 94-0695 (La. 4/28/95), 654 So. 2d 1311.

[75] La. Rev. Stat. § 33:4890.

jurisdiction over ordinances that were enacted in compliance with these and other state preemption provisions.

This article will focus on the general principles based on the rules that govern Lawrason Act mayor's courts. However, the critical distinction between Lawrason and Non-Lawrason charters should first be considered by anyone researching these courts.

PART II

The *De Jure* Rules of the Mayor's Courts

Mayor's courts in Louisiana operate with very little guidance or established rules, and there is little literature written about them. Even references such as the *Mayor's Court Handbook*[76] and *Louisiana Mayor's Court Procedures*[77] admit that there is little state law guidance for the daily operation of these courts. As one court put it, the majority of established rules that exists pertain to either the abolition or establishment of these courts in individual municipalities throughout the state.[78] Likewise, as Part "III.B" of this article explains only a limited number of statutory rules of procedure apply to mayor's courts, which creates the opportunity for procedural due process to be violated.

The few rules that do exist can be put into three categories: rules governing jurisdiction of mayor's courts, rules governing the judicial powers of the mayor, and rules governing appeals of mayor's court decisions. However, these established rules alone do not provide enough of a safeguard to ensure a fair trial. This is mainly because outside of the handful of formal rules that exist a mayor has somewhat

---

[76] Jerry J. Guillot, *Mayor's Court Handbook* 4 (ed. 2013).
[77] David A. Alvarez & Walter W Troxey, *Louisiana Mayor's Court Procedures: Recommendations and Observations* 4 (1971).
[78] *Town of St. Joseph v. Webb*, 46,923 (La. App. 2 Cir. 3/14/12), 87 So. 3d 958, 961, reh'g denied (Apr. 5, 2012), *writ denied,* 2012-1029 (La. 6/22/12), 91 So. 3d 976.

unbridled discretion in how to operate his court, which could differ from other mayor's courts across the state.[79]

This part will identify and clarify the categories of existing rules that govern mayor's courts in Louisiana through four sections so that any limits on authority for these courts can be properly understood. Section "A" will illustrate the rules that establish the jurisdiction of these tribunals. Section "B" will detail the rules that grant mayors authority to prosecute and adjudicate cases. Section "C" will explain why the established codes of procedure do not apply to mayor's courts. Lastly, section "D" will discuss the rules regarding appellate jurisdiction for decisions rendered by mayor's courts.

A. JURISDICTION OF THE MAYOR'S COURTS

Mayor's courts in Louisiana are tribunals with limited jurisdiction. They have jurisdiction to conduct trials, determine guilt, and impose sentences including fines and imprisonment.[80] However, their jurisdiction is limited only to breaches of municipal ordinances that were enacted by the political subdivision where the court is geographically situated.[81] These courts may try breaches of municipal ordinances that are civil or criminal in nature.

Examples of offenses that a mayor's court may handle include traffic violations, violations of zoning ordinances, animal control ordinances, parking ordinances, and electronic or automated enforcement violations (known also as speed and red light camera violations). They may also hear misdemeanor offenses, including for ordinances that mirror state statute violations outlawing the same

---

[79] *Infra.*

[80] *Sledge v. McGlathery*, 324 So. 2d 354, 356 (La. 1975); *State v. Foy*, 401 So. 2d 948, 949 (La. 1981).

[81] Subject matter jurisdiction is set forth in La. Rev. Stat. § 33:441A.(1) which provides: "Except as provided in Chapter 7 of Title 13 of the Louisiana Revised Statutes..., there shall be a mayor's court in the municipality, with jurisdiction over all violations of municipal ordinances. The mayor may try all breaches of the ordinances and impose fines or imprisonment, or both, provided for the infraction thereof."

behavior, as long as there is not special legislation prohibiting it or preempting it.[82] Nevertheless, for both civil and criminal natured violations the offense must be codified as an ordinance by the municipality in order for a mayor's court to have jurisdiction. It should be noted that there is no bright line distinction between which violations are classified as civil or criminal. This classification could vary between cities, and is dependent on factors such as the language of the municipal ordinance, and a city government's intent to make the ordinance civil or punitive in nature.[83]

Mayor's courts do not have subject matter jurisdiction to hear violations of parish law, state law, or any felony, because jurisdiction for these offenses is vested in higher courts.[84] This includes criminal offenses listed in the Criminal Code (Title 14 of the Revised Statutes).[85] Also, mayor's courts lack jurisdiction to hear felonies, because the constitution grants the district courts exclusive original jurisdiction of felony cases.[86] Likewise, the jurisdiction of mayor's courts is secondary to district courts, which have original jurisdiction in all civil and criminal matters.[87] Thus, district courts may hear both violations of municipal ordinances and state statutes, whereas mayor's courts may only hear violations of municipal ordinances and may not hear violations of state statutes.

The jurisdiction of the mayor's court is not exclusive. Mayor's courts have concurrent jurisdiction over violations of municipal ordinances with the district courts. As such, when illegal conduct is prohibited by both a municipal ordinance and a state law, the

---

[82] *Infra.*

[83] For discussion of factors used to distinguish an ordinance as criminal or civil see *Morales v. Parish of Jefferson*, 13-486 (La. App. 5 Cir 04/30/14), 140 So. 3d 375, 384-89.

[84] *See* La. Att'y Gen. Op. No. 2001-0116; 2008 La. AG LEXIS 186.

[85] A crime is that conduct which is defined as criminal in Title 14, or in other acts of the legislature, or in the constitution of this state. La. Rev. Stat. § 14:7. However, note that the definition of "misdemeanor" includes the violation of an ordinance providing a penal sanction. La. Code Crim. Proc. art. 933(4).

[86] La. Const. art. V, § 16(A).

[87] *Id.*

chief of police has the discretion to charge a defendant under either an ordinance or state statute.[88] Hence, the police chief may forward traffic tickets and misdemeanor summonses to either the mayor's court or the parish district attorney. Such discretion is part of the inherent authority and general law enforcement responsibility of the chief of police.[89] Nonetheless, if the police officer arrests or cites for a violation of any state statute, the charges must be referred to the district court.[90]

Moreover, mayor's courts lack jurisdiction to hear cases involving juveniles. This is because the constitution prescribes that special juvenile procedures are to be used for the determination of guilt or innocence, the detention, and the custody of a juvenile.[91] These special procedures are found in the Children's Code, which defines the juvenile jurisdiction of Louisiana's courts. Within this code specific reference is made to special juvenile courts, district courts, parish courts, and city courts, however, no reference to mayor's courts.[92] Additionally, the Children's Code expressly excludes mayor's courts from what it considers as a "court."[93] The term "court" as stated means "any city, parish, district, or juvenile, or its judge, when exercising juvenile jurisdiction as provided for in this Code... It does not include a judge of a mayor's court."[94] Thus, when read

---

[88] La. Att'y Gen. Op. No. 1984-0125.

[89] La. Att'y Gen. Op. No. 1984-0125. Also, the same discretion applies to for sheriff's deputies who issue citations for municipal ordinances within a municipality, and may charge a defendant with either the ordinance or state violation when applicable. La. Att'y Gen. Op. No. 2005-0221.

[90] La. Att'y Gen. Op. 2006-0008; La. Att'y Gen. Op. No. 2011-0129.

[91] The term juvenile in this context refers to a person who is alleged to have committed a crime prior to his seventeenth birthday. La. Const. art. V, § 19. Additionally, the constitution states that "[n]otwithstanding any contrary provision of Section 16 of this Article [District Courts], juvenile and family courts shall have jurisdiction as provided by law." La. Const. art. V, § 18.

[92] La. Child. Code Ann. art. 302.

[93] La. Child. Code Ann. art. 116(4).

[94] *Id.*

together these various provisions clearly indicate that mayor's courts lack juvenile jurisdiction.[95]

Similarly, mayor's courts lack jurisdiction to hear traffic violations charged under the state laws provided in the Louisiana Highway Regulatory Act (Title 32 of the Revised Statutes). However, La. Rev. Stat. § 32:41 permits a municipality to adopt municipal traffic ordinances that do not modify, conflict, or are not inconsistent with Title 32 or state regulations. Any traffic citations issued for a violation of such a municipal traffic ordinance would be within the mayor's court jurisdiction under La. Rev. Stat. § 33:441, and the procedure outlined in La. Rev. Stat. § 32:398.2 clearly indicates that mayor's courts are the proper depository for municipal traffic citations.[96] However, one exception is for violations detailed in La. Rev. Stat. § 14:98 relating to charges of driving while intoxicated (DWI), regardless of whether the defendant is charged under local ordinance, per the directive of La. Rev. Stat. § 13:1894.1.[97] Thus, while mayor's courts may hear municipal violations that mirror state traffic violations, they have no jurisdiction over DWI prosecutions.[98]

B. THE JUDICIAL POWERS OF THE MAYOR

In addition to being the chief executive officer of a municipality, mayors in Louisiana are empowered to exercise a dual judicial role. In this capacity a mayor may both prosecute and determine guilt for violations of municipal ordinances. Additionally, the mayor may assess fines, which in over one-hundred towns makes up a substantial portion of their general fund revenue and in some cases amounts to over a million dollars. This section identifies the laws that allow

---

[95] *See also* La. Att'y. Gen. Op. No. 1996-0116.

[96] La. Att'y Gen. Op. No. 2011-0129; La. Att'y. Gen. Op. No. 2001-0116.

[97] La. Rev. Stat. § 13:1894.1(B) divest jurisdiction in pertinent part under the provision: "mayors' courts shall have no jurisdiction whatsoever over violations as provided for by La. Rev. Stat. § 14:98, nor to the trial of offenses against municipal ordinances relative to prosecutions on charges of driving while intoxicated."

[98] La. Att'y. Gen. Op. No. 2001-0116.

mayors to singlehandedly prosecute, determine guilt, and assess fines. This will be done first by detailing the laws that authorize the mayor to enjoy a judicial role as the presiding officer over the mayor's court. Secondly, this section looks at the laws that allow the mayor to also act as prosecutor in cases he is presiding over.

1. THE MAYOR'S JUDICIAL AUTHORITY TO DETERMINE GUILT AND IMPOSE PENALTIES

In this judicial role the mayor has the power of a committing magistrate, and also enjoys judicial immunity in the same capacity as a judge.[99] All proceedings in mayor's court must be held before the mayor or an attorney appointed to serve as magistrate. As adjudicator, the mayor has authority to try and impose fines or imprisonment or both for violations of ordinances.[100] When a defendant has been convicted, the mayor may suspend the sentence in whole or in part and place the defendant on unsupervised probation with conditions set by the mayor. This probationary period may be imposed for up to six months, but may not exceed the maximum penalty of imprisonment of which may be imposed for violating the ordinance convicted of.[101] However, mayors or their appointed magistrates do

---

[99] La. Rev. Stat. § 33:441.C(1)-(2). The jurisprudence supports immunity for mayor-magistrates, "A judge, of whatever status in the judicial hierarchy, is immune from suit for damages resulting from any act performed in the judicial role." *Meshell v. Town of Zwolle*, CIV.A. 12:00872, 2012 U.S. Dist. LEXIS 113928, 8 (W.D. La. Aug. 10, 2012). It has also been held that immunity also extends to the mayor in his prosecutorial role. *Corley v. Vill. Of Florien*, 2004-853 (La. App. 3 Cir. 12/8/04), 889 So. 2d 364, 366.

[100] La. Rev. Stat. § 33:441.A(1).

[101] La. Rev. Stat. § 33:441.A(3). Note that under La. Rev. Stat. § 33:362.A(2)(b) the maximum penalty for violating an ordinance may be by fine not to exceed five hundred dollars or imprisonment not exceeding sixty days, or both.

not have the authority to suspend sentences so as to place defendants under home incarceration.[102]

The mayor may also impose court costs not to exceed thirty dollars for each convicted offense.[103] The Attorney General's Office has issued an opinion that the mayor has the discretion to impose any amount up to thirty dollars. Since this authority is granted by state statute, any attempt by the board of alderman to limit the amount of court costs that can be assessed by ordinance is preempted by the state statute.[104] In addition, mayor's courts must assess other cost mandated by state statute.[105] Where the imposition of other court costs is not mandated, the mayor or his appointed magistrate has the discretion whether or not to impose these court costs.[106]

---

[102] La. Att'y Gen. Op. No. 1992-0444. Additionally, the authority to place a defendant under home incarceration is provided under La. Code Crim. Proc. art. 894.2. As noted below, mayors' courts are not governed by the Code of Criminal Procedure by way of La. Code Crim. Proc. Ann. art. 931.

[103] La. Rev. Stat. § 33:441.A(1). Note that some municipalities have special legislation allowing for additional court cost to be collected.

[104] La. Att'y Gen. Op. No. 1997-0118.

[105] Examples of additional court fees that apply to mayors' courts include: La. Rev. Stat. § 15:255 (Witness fees to off-duty law enforcement officers); La. Rev. Stat. § 15:1107.6 (Special cost to fund the Feliciana Juvenile Justice District and juvenile detention facility); La. Code Crim. Proc. art. 887.F(1) (Implementation of the master plan for the development of a trial court case management information system); La. Code Crim. Proc. art. 895.4. (Probation; Certified crime stoppers organizations); La. Rev. Stat. § 15:1094.7 (special cost to fund the commission in the parishes of Livingston, St. Helena, St. Tammany, Tangipahoa, and Washington); La. Rev. Stat. § 15:1097.6 (Special cost in the parishes of Bienville, Claiborne, DeSoto, Natchitoches, Red River, Sabine, and Webster; La. Rev. Stat. § 15:1105.6. (Funding for the authority in the parishes within the jurisdiction of the authority); La. Rev. Stat. § 40:2266.1(Jurisdictions with a criminalistics laboratory); La. Rev. Stat. § 15:168. (Judicial district indigent defender fund); La. Rev. Stat. § 33:441.A(1) (Mayor may authorize that a portion of court costs assessed be deposited into a special account and transmitted to the Louisiana Association of Chiefs of Police to be used for law enforcement education and training as required by Louisiana law).

[106] La. Att'y Gen. Op. No. 1993-0538.

Mayors and their appointed magistrates are vested with authority provided under Article V, Section 2 of the Constitution, which states in pertinent part that "[a] judge may issue... all... needful... orders... in aid of the jurisdiction of his court."[107] Appointment of counsel for indigents is one such order because of the mandate in Article I, Section 13 of the Constitution, which holds that "[a]t each stage of the proceedings, every person is entitled to assistance of counsel... appointed by the court if he is indigent and charged with an offense punishable by imprisonment."[108] The U.S. Supreme Court has interpreted the requirement of appointed counsel to apply in instances where a defendant will actually be imprisoned or given a suspended sentence for any offense, whether classified as petty, misdemeanor, or felony.[109] However, appointed counsel is not required for violations where a fine is imposed, or that authorize imprisonment upon conviction but is not actually imposed.[110] Thus, since mayor's courts may punish indigents by actual imprisonment or suspended sentences, the appointment of counsel is a needful writ that may be issued.[111]

The term *"magistrate"* in the context of a mayor's court has been held not to have the same meaning as the term *"judge"*. As one court stated "[i]nsofar as we can determine the term 'judge' has never been applied to mayors who function in mayors' courts... Although the terms 'judge' and 'court' are sometimes used interchangeably, it is clear that mayors...who hold court are, nevertheless, not judges."[112]

---

[107] La. Const. art. V, § 2.

[108] La. Const. art. I, § 13.

[109] *Argersinger v. Hamlin*, 407 U.S. 25, 37 (1972); *Alabama v. Shelton*, 535 U.S. 654, 662 (2002). Consequently, one case study reported that a particular mayor was observed telling defendants in minor cases that it is "not necessary" to have defense counsel. The study further reported that if defendants did not have counsel then the mayor would act as "prosecutor, defense counsel and judge." David A. Alvarez & Walter W Troxey, *Louisiana Mayor's Court Procedures: Recommendations and Observations* 12 (1971).

[110] *Scott v. Illinois*, 440 U.S. 367, 369 (1979).

[111] *Sledge*, 324 So. 2d at 356.

[112] *Broussard v. Town of Delcambre*, 458 So. 2d 1003, 1005 (La. Ct. App. 1984).

Additionally, Article V of the constitution governs matters relating to both "judges" and "courts" but does not treat them as being one in the same.[113] To illustrate this, courts have rejected claims that mayors presiding over the mayor's court violate the constitution because they were not elected as required for all judges under Article V.[114] Likewise, the legislature when describing this position avoided using the term judge, instead chose the words "presiding official over the mayor's court."[115]

There is no requirement that the mayor acting as magistrate be a lawyer, or have attended law school, or have attended any legal training.[116] Constitutional challenges based on the lack of legal training of an untrained adjudicator have been rejected by courts. The U.S. Supreme Court held that "no constitutional violations occur when an accused who is subject to possible imprisonment is tried before a non-lawyer judge when a later trial *de novo* is available."[117] Louisiana meets this requirement by providing the option a *de novo* trial by a district court judge for any mayor's court conviction under La. Rev. Stat. § 13:1896.[118]

Moreover, an additional power of the mayor is that he may request the board of aldermen in its discretion appoint one or more attorneys to be designated as the court magistrate.[119] The mayor is not required

---

[113] *Fonte v. Ansardi*, 493 So. 2d 245, 246-47 (La. Ct. App. 1986).

[114] "The Louisiana Constitution requirement that "all judges be elected" was not meant to cover magistrates appointed to function in mayors' courts." *Broussard v. Town of Delcambre*, 458 So. 2d 1003, 1005 (La. Ct. App. 1984).

[115] *Fonte*, 493 So. 2d at 247.

[116] *In re Cedotal*, 97-1291 (La. 2/6/98), 706 So. 2d 1387, 1390 (Lemmon, J., Concurring).
Note that there is a slight distinction between Louisiana and Ohio. While Ohio does not require that mayors presiding over court be attorneys, they are required to attend 12 hours of training before holding court, and 3 additional hours annually. Ohio Rev. Code § 1905.031 (West); Paul Revelson, *Nothing but Trouble: The Ohio Legislature's Failed Attempts to Abolish Mayor's Courts*, 35 U. Dayton L. Rev. 223, 228 (2010).

[117] *North v. Russell*, 427 U.S. 328, 333-38 (1976).

[118] *Broussard*, 458 So. 2d at 1004.

[119] La. Rev. Stat. § 33:441.B(1).

to request a magistrate be appointed, but if he does it is the board of aldermen who has the authority to make the appointment, and any appointee must be an attorney.[120] Additionally, the appointed magistrate shall serve at the pleasure of the mayor and may from time to time be designated by the mayor to serve in his stead as the presiding official over the mayor's court. Whenever a magistrate is so designated by the mayor to preside over the mayor's court, he shall exercise the powers and authority of the mayor over said court.[121] Since the magistrate serves at the pleasure of the mayor, he is an extension of the mayor, and it is within the mayor's discretion to remove him from the magistrate position.[122]

The Attorney General's Office has issued an opinion that once a magistrate has been appointed to preside over the mayor's court, the mayor retains no concurrent authority with the magistrate over the court.[123] This is because the magistrate acts in place of the mayor, and both cannot preside over the court at the same time. Either one or the other may act at the discretion of the mayor but not both.[124] Likewise, should a magistrate *ad hoc* be appointed, then the mayor relinquishes all authority to preside over those cases. However, note that there is no provision concerning the appointment of a magistrate *ad hoc* to serve as a replacement for the mayor.[125]

The attorney appointed to the magistrate position may also at the same time maintain other employment, such as working in private practice, or as an assistant district or city attorney, or even as a state

---

[120] La. Att'y Gen. Op. No. 2004-0242.

[121] La. Rev. Stat. § 33:441.B(1).

[122] La. Att'y Gen. Op. No. 1993-0313; *Fonte*, 493 So. 2d at 247.

[123] La. Att'y Gen. Op. No. 1993-0313.

[124] La. Att'y Gen. Op. No. 1978-0326.

[125] La. Att'y Gen. Op. No. 1997-0094. Likewise, the Attorney General's Office has issued an opinion that a mayor *pro tem* assuming all duties of the mayor may serve as magistrate. However, the mayor must be truly absent, and it is not sufficient to have a mayor *pro tem* for the mayor's mere convenience or desire. La. Att'y Gen. Op. No. 1985-0330.

legislator.[126] This is because the Louisiana dual officeholding statues (La. Rev. Stat. § 42:61-66) basically only prohibit a full time public employee from holding other full time public employment.[127] When an attorney is appointed as Magistrate of mayor's courts, this position is normally considered a part-time appointed position.[128] Additionally, mayor's courts are considered separate political subdivisions from its municipality and also from district attorneys.[129] Thus, under the dual officeholding laws there would be no conflict of interest if a full time appointed employee, such as an assistant district attorney, was appointed to preside as magistrate.

2. THE MAYOR'S AUTHORITY AS "PROSECUTOR"

In addition to his role as adjudicator, the mayor acts at the same time as prosecutor over proceedings in front of him. As such the mayor may suspend the execution in whole or in part of a fine or imprisonment, or both, and place the defendant on unsupervised or supervised probation up to one year. The probation may be revoked or terminated at any time. Also the probation may include such conditions as the mayor may fix which at any time may be modified, added to, or discharged. At the termination of the probation, the

---

[126] La. Att'y Gen. Op. No. 2004-0201 (state legislator not prohibited); La. Att'y Gen. Op. No. 1985-0228 (town attorney of municipally); La. Att'y Gen. Op. No. 1987-0027 (assistant district attorney).

[127] La. Rev. Stat. § 42:63; La. Att'y Gen. Op. No. 2005-0011.

[128] La. Att'y Gen. Op. No. 2005-0011.

[129] La. Rev. Stat. § 42:62(9) states in pertinent part: "Political subdivision" means a ... municipality." "In addition for the purposes of this Part, mayor's courts... shall be separate political subdivisions." Also note that for purposes of Dual Officeholding, mayor's courts are not within the judicial branch. La. Rev. Stat. § 42:62(8) ("The judicial branch of state government includes all judges, employees, and agents of the supreme court, the judicial administrator, courts of appeal, district courts, including the civil and criminal district courts of Orleans Parish, parish courts, city courts, juvenile and family courts, and any other judicial offices and instrumentalities of the state, but does not include judges or employees of courts not enumerated in this Paragraph").

mayor may set the conviction aside and dismiss the prosecution.[130] Moreover, in his role as prosecutor the mayor or his appointee has the discretion to dismiss or *nolle prosequi* violations presented to the mayor's court, but in his judicial role he can only do so for a legal defect in the proceeding or for insufficient evidence.[131] Also, charges can only be amended by the mayor in his role as prosecutor.[132]

At the outset, La. Const. art. V, § 26(B) provides that the district attorney has "entire charge" of every criminal prosecution by the state in his district.[133] Furthermore, under La. Code Crim. Proc. art. 61 "the district attorney has entire charge and control of every criminal prosecution instituted or pending in his district."[134] However, as Supreme Court Justice Lemmon once noted, the district attorney "has no such control over the prosecutions by the municipality in the mayor's court under municipal ordinances."[135]

Notwithstanding these provisions, the legislature entrusts mayors with both judicial and prosecutorial powers through La. Rev. Stat. § 33:441.A(1) which states "the mayor may try all breaches of... ordinances."[136] Additionally, La. Rev. Stat. § 33:441.B(2) provides that upon the request of the mayor, the board of aldermen in its discretion may appoint one or more attorneys who shall be designated

---

[130] La. Rev. Stat. § 33:441.A(2).

[131] La. Att'y Gen. Op. No. 1989-0665; La. Att'y Gen. Op. No. 1978-1461.

[132] La. Att'y Gen. Op. No. 2006-0075.

[133] La. Const. art. V, § 26(B).

[134] Note that under La. Code Crim. Proc. art. 62B. "The attorney general has authority to institute and prosecute, or to intervene in any proceeding, as he may deem necessary for the assertion or protection of the rights and interests of the state."

[135] *State v. Foy*, 401 So. 2d 948, 951 (La. 1981) (Lemmon, J., Dissenting).

[136] *Corley v. Vill. Of Florien*, 2004-853 (La. App. 3 Cir. 12/8/04), 889 So. 2d 364, 366.

as prosecutor and who shall serve at the pleasure of the mayor.[137] Yet, it has been understood that the mayor is not required to appoint a separate prosecutor and may prosecute all cases him or herself.[138]

Note that the Attorney General's Office has issued the opinion that if the mayor appoints only a prosecutor, then he abandons all of his prosecutorial authority but retains all of this judicial authority. If the mayor appoints both a prosecutor and a magistrate then the mayor maintains neither prosecutorial nor judicial authority because he has delegated away his power to his appointees.[139] Thus, when presiding over court, the mayor maintains both a judicial and a prosecutorial role concurrently unless a designee is appointed.

C. NEITHER CODE OF PROCEDURE APPLIES TO MAYOR'S COURTS

Louisiana has two different codes of procedure: the Louisiana Code of Civil Procedure and the Louisiana Code of Criminal Procedure. However, other than a few exceptions neither of these codes is applicable to mayor's courts. Furthermore, mayor's courts are expressly excluded from having to comply with the Louisiana Code of Evidence.[140] As a result, there is no body of statutory law which governs procedure in these courts.[141]

The Code of Civil Procedure does not mention the term "mayor's court" at all. Furthermore, in Book VIII titled "Trial courts of limited

---

[137] Note that the prosecutor for a mayor's court is a municipal employee and not a municipal officer or municipal attorney. As such the mayor may appoint a prosecutor without the approval of the board of alderman. La. Att'y Gen. Op. No. 2007-0216. However, the prosecutor can only get paid if his salary is budged by the board of alderman. *See* La. Rev. Stat. § 39:1301 *et. seq.* (Louisiana Local Government Budget Act); "The board of aldermen shall fix and pay the salary of each prosecutor, if any are appointed." La. Rev. Stat. § 33:441.B(2).

[138] *Corley v. Vill. Of Florien*, 2004-853 (La. App. 3 Cir. 12/8/04), 889 So. 2d 364, 366.

[139] La. Att'y Gen. Op. No. 2006-0008.

[140] *Infra.*

[141] *State v. Fontenot*, 535 So. 2d 433, 436-37 (La. Ct. App. 1988).

jurisdiction", La. Code Civ. Proc. art. 4832 expressly states that trial courts of limited jurisdiction are parish courts, city courts, and justice of the peace courts, but does not mention mayor's courts.[142] Additionally, Book VIII specifically provides jurisdiction for parish courts, city courts, and justice of the peace court, and also appellate procedure from decisions of these courts, but again does not mention mayor's courts.[143] Hence, it would appear that the legislature did not intend for the Code of Civil Procedure to apply to civil proceedings before the mayor's court. Consequently, under Louisiana's civilian tradition, it's unknown whether mayor's courts would be required to follow precedent or "common law doctrines" in adjudicating civil matters.

The Code of Criminal Procedure, and its ancillaries in Title 15, in general does not apply to mayor's courts. La. Code Crim. Proc. art. 15 states the courts that the provisions in the code apply to, namely district, city, parish, juvenile, and family courts, but does not include mayor's courts. Additionally, La. Code Crim. Proc. Ann. art. 931 expressly excludes mayor's courts from definition of "court" and "city court", however it does include a mayor of a mayor's court in the definition of a "magistrate".[144] It is through this classification of a magistrate that a few exceptions in Code of Criminal Procedure are possible. The exceptions where this code may apply include: the

---

[142] La. Code Civ. Proc. art. 4832.

[143] La. Code Civ. Proc. art. 4924 *et seq.*; La. Code Civ. Proc. art. 5001 *et seq.*

[144] La. Code Crim. Proc. art. 931. Courts, judges, and magistrates. Except where the context clearly indicates otherwise, as used in this Code:

    (1) "Court" means a court with criminal jurisdiction or its judge. It does not include a mayor's court or a justice of the peace.

    (2) "City court" means a city, town, village, or other municipal court, with criminal jurisdiction. It does not include a mayor's court or a justice of the peace.

    (3) "Judge" means a judge of a court, as defined in this article.

    (4) "Magistrate" means any judge, a justice of the peace, or a mayor of a mayor's court.

Comment (a) states that "the definition expressly excludes a justice of the peace and a mayor's court, which are all tribunals with very limited criminal jurisdiction."

authority to set bail, order peace bonds, issue arrest warrants, issuing probable cause affidavits, and punishing for contempt.[145]

However, apart from for these five possible exceptions, the Code of Criminal Procedure does not apply to mayor's courts, nor do these courts have to comply with this code.[146] To further illustrate this point, if the code were applicable then mayor's courts would have to comply with all of its provisions. This would include having to produce a record of trial proceedings under La. Code Crim. Proc. art. 777, yet mayor's courts are not required to do this because they

---

[145] Exceptions where the Code of Criminal Procedure apply include:

- Setting bail: "The following magistrates... shall have authority to fix bail: (3) Mayor's courts and traffic courts in criminal cases within their trial jurisdiction." La. Code Crim. Proc. art. 333(3). *See* also La. Rev. Stat. § 15:81. (Bond for release for violation of municipal ordinances).

- Peace Bonds: "A magistrate may order a peace bond in conformity with the provisions of this Chapter." La. Code Crim. Proc. art. 26. "The peace bond obligation shall run... in favor of the city when ordered by the mayor of a mayor's court." La. Code Crim. Proc. art. 30.C.

- Issuing arrest warrants: "A warrant of arrest may be issued by any magistrate." *see* La. Code Crim. Proc. Ann. art. 202. Additionally, La. Code Crim. Proc. art. 931 comment (d) states "The definition of "magistrate" is ...broad enough to cover any officer who has authority to issue warrants of arrest or order peace bonds." Note that because of the potential for bias by mayor-judges, the authority to issue warrants by mayors should be questioned. As the U.S. Supreme Court noted, the signing and issuance of arrest warrants is to be undertaken only by a "neutral and detached" judicial officer. *Coolidge v. New Hampshire*, 403 U.S. 443, 449 (1971).

- Issuing probable cause affidavits: Law enforcement officers making an arrest without warrant to submit a probable cause affidavit to a magistrate. *See* La. Code Crim. Proc. Ann. art. 230.2.

- The Attorney General's Office has issued the opinion that mayor's courts may punish for contempt of court pursuant to the inherit powers under La. Code Crim. Proc. art. 16 *et seq.* La. Att'y Gen. Op. No. 1998-235 P28. However, the Code of Criminal Procedure states that as an inherent authority "[a] *court* has the power to punish for contempt," yet under La. Code Crim. Proc. art. 931 mayor's courts are expressly excluded from the term "court" in the code.

[146] *Id.*; *City of Kenner v. Marquis*, 98-418 (La. App. 5 Cir. 6/4/98), 715 So. 2d 85, 87 *writ denied,* 98-1806 (La. 10/16/98), 726 So. 2d 907.

are not courts of record.[147] Moreover, if this code were applicable to mayor's courts, then the procedure for appeals would be governed under La. Code Crim. Proc. art. 911 *et seq.*, and not under La. Rev. Stat. § 13:1896A. More importantly, no binding authority has held that mayor's courts are governed under the Code of Criminal Procedure (or the Code of Civil Procedure).

Assuming *arguendo* that the Code of Criminal Procedure is applicable to mayor's courts, the extent of its applicability is unanswered and has been the source of confusion for many. One of the reasons for the misconception stems from the 1967 case of *Harahan v. Olson.*[148] In *Olson* the Supreme Court was presented with a challenge on whether a mayor's court could prohibit a citizen from violating a civil zoning ordinance by issuing an injunction. In holding that mayor's courts do not have the authority to grant injunctive relief, the court stated that it believed enforcement of city ordinances could only be done through criminal proceedings.[149] However, the court did not mention anything about the applicability of the Code of Criminal Procedure.

Following *Olson*, some courts and also the Attorney General's Office began looking to specific articles in the Code of Criminal Procedure for guidance on issues. This was likely done pursuant to La. Code Crim. Proc. art. 3, which states "[w]here no procedure

---

[147] Pleas shall be immediately entered in the minutes of the court. *See* La. Code Crim. Proc. art. 553A; *see also* La. Rev. Stat. § 13:961(C); *State v. Fontenot*, 535 So. 2d 433, 438 (La. Ct. App. 1988).

[148] *City of Harahan v. Olson*, 250 La. 999, 200 So. 2d 874 (1967).

[149] *Id.*, 250 La. 1002-03, 200 So. 2d 875. Prior to *Olson*, the Supreme Court had held that municipalities could not substitute criminal proceedings to enforcement of payment for licenses, when the legislature has provided that these proceedings shall be of a civil nature. *Town of Abita Springs v. Pons*, 145 La. 990, 992-93, 83 So. 216, 217 (1919). Furthermore, "[t]he course of procedure before a mayor's court is summary. Proceedings for the punishment of offenders against municipal ordinances enacted in virtue of implied or incidental powers of corporations, or in the exercise of legitimate police authority for the preservation of peace, good order, safety and health, and which relate to minor acts and matters, are not usually or properly regarded as criminal." *State ex rel. Courrege v. Fisher*, 50 La. Ann. 45, 47, 23 So. 92, 93 (1898).

is specifically prescribed by this Code or by statute, the *court* may proceed in a manner consistent with the spirit of the provisions of this Code and other applicable statutory and constitutional provisions." (Emphasis added). As a result, some lower courts may have treated the Code of Criminal Procedure as though it is binding on mayor's courts, and issued opinions inconsistent with the *jurisprudence constante* of other Louisiana courts. However, it is critical to note that article 3 only applies to the "court", and under La. Code Crim. Proc. art. 931 mayor's courts are expressly excluded from the term "court" in the code.

One additional thing to note about the lack of formal rules is that the Louisiana Code of Evidence does not apply to mayor's courts. This is because the Code of Evidence expressly excludes them.[150] However, the underlying principles of this code serve as "guides" to the admissibility of evidence in all proceedings before mayor's courts.[151]

D. APPEAL AS A QUASI-SAFEGUARD TO MAYOR'S COURT DECISIONS

The law provides the option of appealing to the district courts as a quasi-safeguard against due process violations that could result from mayor's court decisions.[152] However, this safeguard may come with added expenses that could discourage convicted defendants from using it. The extra expenses for bring an appeal is distinguished by whether the offense convicted of is criminal or civil in nature.

The procedure for appealing from a mayor's court decision in a *criminal* case is provided in La. Rev. Stat. § 13:1896. Under this

---

[150] La. Code Evid. Ann. art. 1101B. states "[e]xcept as otherwise provided by Article 1101(A)(2) and other legislation, in the following proceedings, the principles underlying this Code shall serve as guides to the admissibility of evidence. The specific exclusionary rules and other provisions, however, shall be applied only to the extent that they tend to promote the purposes of the proceeding.... (5) All proceedings before mayors' courts and justice of the peace courts."

[151] *Id.*

[152] *See* also La. Const. art. I, § §19. (Constitutional right to judicial review).

provision district courts have appellate jurisdiction over all criminal convictions rendered by a mayor's court or justice of the peace courts where the defendant was subjected to imprisonment or forfeiture of rights or property. The appeals made to the district court shall be tried *de novo*.[153] This statute also provides that the time for taking an appeal for a criminal conviction follows the time provided in the Code of Criminal Procedure, which is 30 days after judgment is rendered by the mayor's court.[154] Note that the actual method for taking an appeal is not stated in La. Rev. Stat. § 13:1896, although the Attorney General's Office issued an opinion that a motion for an appeal may be made orally in open court or by filing a written motion with the clerk.[155]

The law is somewhat vague on whether there exists any procedure for appealing a *civil* judgment issued by a mayor's court as there is no governing statutory provision for this.[156] However, the Louisiana Court of Appeals for the Third Circuit has held that the trial *de novo* applies to civil proceedings in mayor's courts.[157] Moreover, this same court later noted that the proper procedure when appealing a criminal conviction from the mayor's court is through a trial *de novo* under La. Rev. Stat. § 13:1896, and not to initiate a civil suit for illegal conviction and motion to quash in district court. The court reasoned that any motion to quash or issues of due process would be heard in the district court at that time. Criminal procedural protocol (such as La. Rev. Stat. § 13:1896) exists to catch errors and avoid civil

---

[153] La. Rev. Stat. § 13:1896(1).

[154] La. Rev. Stat. § 13:1896(2); La. Code Crim. Proc. art. 914; *see* La. Code Crim. Proc. art. 881.1.

[155] La. Att'y Gen. Op. No. 1999-0294; *see* La. Code Crim. Proc. art. 914.

[156] Note that the appeal procedure for criminal convictions from *both* mayor's and justice of the peace courts is provided in La. Rev. Stat. § 13:1896A. However, the comparable appeal procedure from civil cases is only exists for justice of the peace courts. La. Code Civ. Proc. art. 4924-25.

[157] *City of Broussard v. Watkins*, 2003-1383 (La. App. 3 Cir. 3/31/04), 869 So. 2d 962, 968. See also La. Rev. Stat. § 33:4788 (Appeals from [civil] suspension or revocation of permit).

suits against mayor's courts that would result whenever a would-be appellant receives an unfavorable result.[158]

Where the defendant appeals a judgment from a mayor's court, the general rule is that the district court is to try the case without regard to the previous decision. The appeal is to be heard as if it originally commenced in the district court. Furthermore, the district court's is to enter its own independent judgment. The one exception is that the district court is limited to the penalty assessed by the mayor's court and may not issue a more severe sentence, but may issue a lesser one.[159]

Unique to convictions from mayor's courts is the ability to appeal for a trial *de novo* from guilty *pleas* made by a defendant (in addition to guilty verdicts).[160] The reason for allowing this is to insure that defendants are afforded procedural safeguards to protect their constitutional rights. This is because defendants before a mayor's court are not protected by any code of criminal procedure, which are designed to protect a defendant's constitutional rights.[161] Similarly, since mayor's courts are not courts of record there will normally be no way for the district court hearing the appeal to determine whether constitutional guarantees were met.[162] Without any transcript of the hearing before the mayor, the district courts will be unable to inspect any record to see whether the defendant's guilty plea was knowingly and voluntarily made. Furthermore, there won't be any evidence showing whether the defendant was properly advised of

---

[158] *Glass v. City of Oberlin*, 2012-414 (La. App. 3 Cir. 11/7/12), 2012 La. App. Unpub. LEXIS 691, p4, 116 So. 3d 113 *writ not considered*, 2012-2688 (La. 2/8/13), 107 So. 3d 640.

[159] *Town of St. Joseph v. Webb*, 46,923 (La. App. 2 Cir. 3/14/12), 87 So. 3d 958, 962, reh'g denied (Apr. 5, 2012), *writ denied*, 2012-1029 (La. 6/22/12), 91 So. 3d 976.

[160] *Fontenot*, 535 So. 2d at 437.

[161] *Id.* at 437-38.

[162] The only recording requirements provided by statute are that "[t]he mayor shall keep a regular docket, on which he shall enter the causes arising under the ordinances and to be tried by him. He shall keep a perfect record of all cases tried." La. Rev. Stat. § 33:442.

his rights prior to entering the plea.[163] Accordingly, to guarantee that defendants' rights are observed, appeals *de novo* are allowed for both guilty verdicts and guilty pleas from mayor's courts.

This option of appeal should be considered only a quasi-safeguard against due process violations. This is because if the district court finds a defendant not guilty then he does not have to pay the fines that had been assessed by the mayor. Notwithstanding, an appeal *de novo* will still offer more due process protection because the district judges is less likely to be biased than a mayors since they have no connection to a city's general funds, and also the codes of procedure apply to these cases heard in district court. However, appellants for civil natured violations will likely have to pay expensive court cost up front to the district court to bring an appeal which inevitably cost more than the mayor assessed fine itself.

There is some uncertainty in determine court cost of appealing a decision rendered by a mayor's court because neither the Revised Statutes nor La. Rev. Stat. § 13 specifically account for these types of appeals from mayor's courts in its fee schedules.[164] Courts distinguish court costs and filing fees on whether the offense is civil or criminal in nature. The difference being that filing a civil appeal could likely cost several hundred dollars up front as it will need to be filed as a new suit, whereas court cost in a criminal appeal are assessed post conviction and are not as extreme.[165] For example, to appeal a civil judgment from the mayor's court in the City of Gretna (Jefferson Parish) would cost $400 just to file a new suit at the 24th Judicial District Court.[166]

---

[163] *Fontenot*, 535 So. 2d at 438.

[164] Also note also the semantics problem with the term mayor's court in La. Rev. Stat. § 13 and its exclusion from the term "court" as described in Part "II.C" above.

[165] *See* La. Rev. Stat. § 13:841 *et seq.* Also, *see* La. Code. Civ. Proc. art. 4857 which was enacted as special legislation in New Orleans so that appeals for automated traffic enforcement violations could be directed to the New Orleans Traffic Court instead of paying expensive court cost to file a new suit in Civil District Court.

[166] http://www.jpclerkofcourt.us/fees/.

PART III

Two Constitutional Problems Defendant's Encounter

This part details the two problems with mayor's courts that jeopardize procedural due process. Section "A" shows how there is an inherent possible temptation for mayors to rule more favorably against defendants. Section "B" explains the risk to due process that results from the lack of formal procedural rules. Lastly, section "C" provides prospective solutions to both constitutional problems presented.

A. CONSTITUTIONAL CHALLENGE 1: DENIAL OF THE RIGHT TO TRIAL BY A NEUTRAL DECISIONMAKER

The first constitutional problem that defendants before a mayor's court face is the possibility that the mayor presiding over court is predetermined to rule against them. This is because the mayor's dual executive role compels a responsibility to raise money for the city, which includes fines assessed from guilty judgments. This threatens the Due Process Clause's protection that entitles a person to a hearing by an impartial and disinterested judge in both civil and criminal cases. This requirement of neutrality in adjudicative proceedings helps safeguard that no person will be deprived of his life, liberty, or property interests by a judge that is not predisposed to find against him.[167]

The U.S. Supreme Court has recognized that the potential for bias exists for mayor presiding over court when they have a financial

---

[167] *Marshall v. Jerrico, Inc.*, 446 U.S. 238, 242 (1980).

34

interest in the outcome of the case.[168] This is especially true when fines being assessed account for a substantial portion of a city's general fund revenue. Notwithstanding, several mayor's courts across Louisiana continue to assess fines that contribute substantial amounts of income. To illustrate this problem the first section of this part will detail the U.S. Supreme Court precedent addressing the issue of neutrality in mayor's courts. The second section will detail how the state of Ohio has further interpreted the U.S. Supreme Court's decisions. Lastly, the third section will illustrate how mayor's courts in Louisiana jeopardize procedural due process by not comporting with these court decisions.

1. THE U.S. SUPREME COURT PRECEDENT IGNORED BY MAYOR'S COURTS

One of the leading cases to address this issue is *Tumey v. Ohio*.[169] In *Tumey*, the U.S. Supreme Court held that a defendant's Fourteenth Amendment right to due process was denied after he was convicted by a mayor in the mayor court for a village in Ohio.[170] The defendant's claim was that the mayor had a pecuniary interest in ruling against him. This was because under state law the mayor could only be compensated for his role as judge from fines received for convictions in matters that came before him. The U.S. Supreme Court held that "it certainly... deprives a defendant in a criminal case of due process of law, to subject his liberty or property to the judgment of a court the judge of which has a direct, personal, substantial, pecuniary interest in reaching a conclusion against him in his case."[171]

The court then provided the test for determining whether a mayor could be a fair arbiter. The question under this test is whether the mayor's situation is one "which would offer a *possible temptation* to the average man as a judge to forget the burden of proof required

---

[168] *Infra.*

[169] *Tumey v. Ohio*, 273 U.S. 510 (1927).

[170] *Id.* at 523.

[171] *Id.*

to convict the defendant, or which might lead him not to hold the balance nice, clear and true between the State and the accused...."[172] (Emphasis added). Due Process was violated because the Ohio law created a "possible temptation" which could make the mayor partisan so as to maintain the high level of revenue from the mayor's court.[173]

Additionally, in reaching its conclusion the *Tumey* Court also focused on the role of the mayor as the chief executive of the village. As chief executive, a mayor has the duty to look after the village finances, and cannot escape this representative capacity.[174] The court stated that "[a] situation in which an official perforce occupies two practically and seriously inconsistent positions, one partisan and the other judicial, necessarily involves a lack of due process of law in the trial of defendants charged with crimes before him."[175] However, the court noted that the "the mere union of the executive power and the judicial power in him cannot be said to violate due process of law" where minor penalties or judgments of a mayor "do not involve any such additional revenue of the village as to justify the fear that the mayor would be influenced in his judicial judgment by that fact."[176]

In further contemplating the dual role of a mayor, the U.S. Supreme Court in *Dugan v. Ohio* suggested that a crucial consideration is the remoteness of the pecuniary interest alleged to be the biasing influence.[177] In *Dugan*, after being convicted by the mayor in the city's mayor's court, the defendant questioned the impartiality of the mayor based on his dual role as arbitrator and chief executor of the city. The court held that due process is not violated in circumstances in which the mayor had no executive duties, even though he has judicial power to convict and impose fines.[178] Under the city's charter the mayor was one of the five city commissioners who together

---

[172] *Id.*

[173] *Id.*

[174] *Id.* at 533.

[175] *Id.* at 534.

[176] *Id.*

[177] *Dugan v. Ohio*, 277 U.S. 61, 65 (1928).

[178] *Id.* at 65.

exercised legislative functions, and the executive functions were executed by a separate manager. The mayor was a member of the city commission which fixed his salary, but only the other members of the commission could vote in the matter. The court held in this case that the mayor's relationship to the finances and financial policy of the city was too remote to warrant a presumption of bias in the mayor's role as judge.[179]

The next case on this issue was *Ward v. Monroeville*.[180] In *Ward* the U.S. Supreme Court was again faced a due process challenge regarding the impartiality of a mayor in his dual role as chief executor and arbitrator. In this case an Ohio mayor's court operated under a process where the mayor acted as judge and levied fines that were paid into the village treasury.[181] The mayor did not directly receive any part of his salary from the fines, but was responsible for the conducting and financing of village affairs.[182] Nevertheless, the court held that due process had been violated because the fines produced from the mayor's court accounted for a "major part" of municipal revenues. The reasoning was that the desire to maintain a "high level of contribution" from the mayor's court is a "forbidden temptation" under the test provided in *Tumey*, which could make the mayor partisan.[183]

The *Ward* Court published in its opinion the amount of fines collected and the amount of village income collected for the years 1964 thru 1968, which the court determined to be high enough of a level of contribution to create a "possible temptation." Those figures, along with the percentage that the fines comprise the income of the village are as follows:

---

[179] *Id.*
[180] *Ward v. Monroeville*, 409 U.S. 57 (1972).
[181] *Id.* at 58 n.1.
[182] *Id.* at 58.
[183] *Id.* at 60.

TABLE 2[184]

Year	Fines collected	Village Income	% of Income
1964	$23,590	$46,355	50.88%
1965	$18,509	$46,753	39.58%
1966	$16,085	$43,585	36.90%
1967	$20,061	$53,931	37.19%
1968	$23,439	$52,996	44.22%

* Values rounded to nearest dollar.

Moreover, the *Ward* Court rejected the contention that any unfairness could be corrected on appeal by a trial *de novo* in the county court. Adding that "[t]his 'procedural safeguard' does not guarantee a fair trial in the mayor's court; there is nothing to suggest that the incentive to convict would be diminished by the possibility of reversal on appeal."[185] The Court also stated that a defendant in mayor's court is "entitled to a neutral and detached judge in the first instance," and rejected the argument that the trial court procedure should be deemed constitutional simply because he is eventually offered an impartial adjudication.[186]

2. OHIO'S INTERPRETATION OF *TUMEY* AND *WARD*

Following the holdings by the U.S. Supreme Court, Ohio courts were presented with challenges to the constitutionality of mayor's courts there. As noted above, Ohio is the only other state in the country that continues to operate mayor's courts in their municipalities. The Ohio jurisprudence that further interprets the U.S. Supreme Court precedent is provided in the cases of *Rose v. Village of Peninsula* and *DePiero v. City of Macedonia*.[187]

---

[184] *Id.* at 58.

[185] *Id.* at 62.

[186] *Id.* at 62-63.

[187] *Rose v. Vill. of Peninsula*, 875 F. Supp. 442 (N.D. Ohio 1995); *DePiero v. City of Macedonia*, 180 F.3d 770 (6th Cir. 1999).

In *Rose*, a challenge was brought after a mayor have the speed limit signs changed on a state highway from 50 m.p.h. to 35 m.p.h. without receiving authorization from the Ohio Dept. of Transportation (ODOT).[188] Under state law the speed limit could be changed for safety reasons, but only with permission of the ODOT.[189] After being convicted for speeding by the mayor, the defendant alleged that the motivation for lowering the speed limit was not for safety reasons, but instead was a ploy to create a "speed trap" for the purpose of increasing village revenue.[190]

In his defense, the mayor pointed out that the fines collected for the preceding three years only ranged from 11.8% to 13.9% of total general fund revenue (see TABLE 3 for amounts).[191] Although the fines averaged only 10% of the total revenue, the court held that this was "substantial" both in the absolute amount and as a percentage of total revenue enough to make up a major part of the village revenue as in *Ward*.[192] Additionally, it made no difference that the majority of convictions came from guilty pleas, or the fact that only 0.25% of the total general funds came from contested violations.[193] This is because it was the amounts collected from *all* fines that created the fear of impartiality in *Ward*, not just contested fines or even acquittal rates.[194] The *Rose* Court further stated that "certainly, any person

---

[188] *Rose*, 875 F. Supp. at 444-45.

[189] *Id.* at 445.

[190] *Id.*

[191] *Id.* at 451.

TABLE 3	Year	Fine Revenue	Total General Fund Revenue	% of Income
	1990	$ 49,560.00	$ 402,236.00	12.3%
	1991	$ 65,627.20	$ 558,378.00	11.8%
	1992	$ 72,549.51	$ 521,099.00	13.9%

[192] *Id.* at 450-51.

[193] *Id.* at 451.

[194] *Id.*

suddenly deprived on 10% or more of his income would find the loss 'substantial.'"[195]

However, while "substantiality" is an important factor, the principal question is whether the mayor "occupies two practically and seriously inconsistent positions, one partisan and the other judicial."[196] On the outset, the more substantial the amount or percentage of fine revenue collected from a mayor's court, the more reasonable it is to question the impartiality of a mayor who has any executive authority. In similar fashion, the more executive authority vested in a mayor, the more reasonable it is to question the impartiality of a mayor who produced even a relatively small amount of revenue through a mayor's court. Thus, inadequate separation of powers in a mayor-judge may occur despite the mayor's court's collection of a fairly insignificant percentage of general fund revenue.[197]

The *Rose* Court further noted that a mayor as executive officer appoints the chief of police and police officers, and as a judge he evaluates their credibility as against opposing witnesses.[198] As a result, there is good reason for keeping separate the executive power of appointment of police officers and the judicial power of evaluating their credibility. This is because it is exceedingly difficult for an average mayor to wear both of these hats and still dispense justice which satisfies the appearance of justice.[199]

A few years later in *DePiero* the issue of partiality was again raised regarding a mayor's dual executive and judicial role.[200] Even though fines in this case made up only 4% of the city's total revenue, the broad executive powers that the mayor possessed had created a situation for him to be biased.[201] As chief executor of the city, one

---

[195] *Id.*

[196] *Id.* at 451. (quoting *Ward*, 409 U.S. at 60).

[197] *Id.* at 451.

[198] *Id.* (citing *Vill. of Monroeville v. Ward*, 27 Ohio St. 2d 179, 193(1971) (Corrigan, J. dissenting) *rev'd sub nom. Ward v. Vill. of Monroeville*, 409 U.S. 57(1972).

[199] *Id.* at 452.

[200] *DePiero v. City of Macedonia*, 180 F.3d 770 (6th Cir. 1999).

[201] *Id.* at 780-82.

of his duties was to appoint a police chief for the city. As such, the "possible temptation" existed for the mayor to forgo the burden of proof and give credence to the testimony of police officers, which the mayor had ultimate appointment responsibility.[202] The court held that the mere possibility of temptation to ignore the burden of proof is all that is required, and actual temptation or bias is not needed.[203] As a result of *DePiero* mayors with any type executive power will likely be deemed partial, even if only a small percentage of total revenue comes from fines.

It should be noted that following these cases, the Ohio Courts Futures Commission recommended to the Ohio Supreme Court that the role of mayor's courts should be assumed by trial courts.[204] This recommendation was based on a three year study by the commission which found that the absence or lack of legal training by mayor-magistrates was far from comparable to the legal education required for judges of other courts.[205] The commission also found that an apparent conflict of interest existed when the mayor possessed the dual role of executive officer of a city and also levies fines in mayor's court that are used to support the city government.[206] Additionally, in 2007 the 127th Ohio General Assembly unsuccessfully tried on three separate occasions to legislatively abolish or limit the mayor's courts, but each attempt was never fully voted on.[207]

3. THE CONSTITUTIONAL PROBLEM IN LOUISANA

The lack of procedural safeguards and mandatory reporting requirements has enabled mayors in Louisiana the opportunity to act in ways that goes against U.S. Supreme Court precedent. This

---

[202] *Id.* at 782.

[203] *Id.*

[204] *A Changing Landscape*, Ohio Courts Futures Commission Report, 50 (2000).

[205] *Id.* at 11, 32.

[206] *Id.* at 53.

[207] Paul Revelson, *Nothing but Trouble: The Ohio Legislature's Failed Attempts to Abolish Mayor's Courts*, 35 U. Dayton L. Rev. 223, 234-35 (2010).

section will first will point out the inherent conflict of interests that exists with mayors having dual executive and judicial roles. Secondly, this section will illustrate how several mayor's courts collect fine amounts that exceed the established constitutional limitations.

First, it is important to note that many features of mayors in Louisiana are similar to the aspects of Ohio mayors which were struck down as unconstitutional in the above cases. For instance, mayors in Louisiana occupy the dual role as both the chief executive officer of a municipality, and a judicial role as presiding officer over mayor's court.[208] In doing this mayors in Louisiana occupy two practically and seriously inconsistent positions, one partisan and the other judicial. As noted in *Tumey*, this unavoidably creates a situation where it will always be reasonable to question the impartiality of mayors in their judicial role.

Additionally, Louisiana law allows for mayors to appoint the chief of police in number of municipalities, and to have supervisory control over such police departments.[209] Nonetheless, even in municipalities that have an elected chief of police, the law still provides that the mayor has some control over the hiring, promoting, disciplining, and terminating of police personnel.[210] In similar fashion, the mayor maintains control over the police as he is responsible for submitting an

---

[208] La. Rev. Stat. § 33:362.B (executive role); La. Rev. Stat. § 33:441 (judicial role).
[209] The mayor and chief of police in all municipalities shall be elected at large... Municipalities where the chief of police is appointed rather than elected as of August 1, 1970, may continue to operate with an appointive chief. La. Rev. Stat. § 33:381.B; La. Rev. Stat. § 33:381.1. (Provisions for appointing a marshal who acts as the chief of police); La. Rev. Stat. § 33:381.2. (Provisions for the election or appointment of marshal in municipalities of five thousand or less); The mayor shall have the powers, duties, and responsibilities to supervise and direct the administration and operation of all municipal departments, offices, and agencies, other than a police department with an elected chief of police. La. Rev. Stat. § 33:404.A.(1).
[210] "In those municipalities governed by the provisions of the [Lawrason Act] which have a chief of police elected by the qualified voters thereof, he shall make recommendations to the mayor and board of aldermen for appointment of police personnel, for the promotion of officers, to effect disciplinary action, and for dismissal of police personnel." La. Rev. Stat. § 33:423.A.

annual budget, which includes salaries for police officers. Therefore, the possible temptation may exist for mayors presiding over court to more favorably weigh the creditability of police officers who testify as witnesses against defendants.

The second factor to consider is the percentage of fine revenue that makes up the total general revenue of a municipality. This is an important consideration since the mayor in his executive capacity has a fiscal responsibility to maintain a budget, which is a duty that is central to the role of mayor and cannot be disregarded.[211] Because of this financial obligation, the jurisprudence above directs that whenever the fines collected from a mayor's court amount to a major part of a municipality's general revenue, it is reasonable to question the neutrality of the mayor presiding over court.[212] The reason being that the inherent desire to produce more revenue from fines creates a "possible temptation" that would cause an average mayor to decide cases more favorably against defendants. While the U.S. Supreme Court did not say what a safe percentage level would be, it did affirmatively hold that the levels presented in *Ward*, which began at 36%, constituted a major part of the village revenue. Additionally, *Rose* held that 10% of total general fund revenue was substantial enough to create a "possible temptation."

In order to assess compliance with this mandate, TABLE 1 (see appendix) presents a list of one-hundred municipalities with mayor's courts that collected fines in excess of the ten percent threshold during their 2013 fiscal year. TABLE 1 also provides the total amount of fines collected compared to the amount of total general fund revenue collected by its municipality, and also the percentage that the fines comprise of total general fund revenue.

A comparative analysis of TABLE 1 and TABLE 2 shows that many Louisiana mayor's courts collect percentages of fines

---

[211] Mayor has duty to prepare and submit an annual operations budget ... for the municipality to the board of aldermen in accordance with the provisions of La. Rev. Stat. § 39:1301 *et seq.* and any other supplementary laws or ordinances. La. Rev. Stat. § 33:404(5).

[212] *Supra.*

that are similar to and far exceeded the percentage amounts held unconstitutional in *Ward* and *Rose*. As TABLE 1 shows, several mayor's courts in Louisiana continue to operate with complete disregard of established precedent. A few examples from the 2013 fiscal year include the Village of Georgetown collecting 94% of his general fund revenue from fines, the Village of Fenton collecting 89% of its general revenue from fines, and the City of Gretna collecting over $5.3 million dollars from fines.[213] If the "possible temptation" was held to exist in Ohio mayors with ratios of 10%, then by analogy the same "possible temptation" exists with mayors in Louisiana. Thus, the inherent financial responsibility of Louisiana mayors creates the probable temptation to pass a predisposed judgment against defendants so as to increase general fund revenues.

Despite the U.S. Supreme Court precedent, the lack of oversight over mayor's courts allows the opportunity for some courts to habitually violate the Fourteenth Amendment. As a result, many people may be wrongfully convicted by impartial mayors or be forced to undergo extra hassle and expense of obtaining a fair and impartial trial (appeal) by a district court. For some defendants, they may realize that the cost of appeal far outweighs the cost of just paying the fines. Instead of appealing from the mayor's court they may simply chose to accept a wrongful conviction that violates their rights rather than having to put up extra court cost, attorney's fees, or take off more days from work to attend court. Furthermore, the U.S. Supreme Court has noted that while some mayors would not let such consideration affect their judgment, due process "may sometimes bar trial by judges who have no actual bias and would do their very best to weigh the scales of justice."[214] Thus, because of the possible temptations that exist for mayors to adjudicate unfairly, in order to protect the liberty and property interest of defendants additional safeguards need to be implemented.

---

[213] See Table 1 (Appendix).

[214] *Caperton v. A.T. Massey Coal Co., Inc.*, 556 U.S. 868, 886 (2009); *see Tumey*, 273 U.S. at 532.

B. CONSTITUTIONAL CHALLENGE 2: THE LACK OF FORMAL PROCEDURAL RULES HAVE LED TO ARBITRARY PROCEDURES

One of the primary purposes for codes of procedure and laws governing courts is to protect the constitutional rights of parties having matters adjudicated. As noted above, the only provisions pertaining to mayor's courts are the Constitution which recognizes their existence, the Lawrason Act governing its jurisdiction, La. Rev. Stat. § 13:1896 governing appeals, and random snippets of rules located in various statute books. A problem with mayor's courts is that besides having very little statutory guidance for daily functions, there are very few procedural rules applicable to them. Consequently this gap in the law has likely caused confusion amongst the courts and may lead to inconsistent rulings. As a result, the ability to get a fair trial is hindered, and the potential exists for the guarantee of procedural due process of law to be denied.

Due process of law is a right guaranteed under both the U.S. Constitution and the Louisiana Constitution.[215] Courts have held that the term "due process of law," when applied to judicial proceedings, means a course of legal proceedings according to established rules regulating judicial proceedings.[216] As such the "touchstone" of procedural due process is the protection against arbitrary action of the government, and the goal of due process analysis is to determine whether the state has provided adequate procedures to minimize efficiently the risk of arbitrary or erroneous deprivations of life, liberty or property.[217] The U.S. Supreme Court once said that due process of the law is secured when people subject to legislation are treated alike under similar circumstances and conditions.[218]

---

[215] U.S. Const. art. V; U.S. Const. art. XIV, § 1; La. Const. art. I, § 2 (Due Process of Law); See also La. Const. art. I § 16 (Right to a Fair Trial).

[216] *Pettit v. Penn*, 180 So. 2d 66, 69 (La. Ct. App. 1965) *writ refused,* 248 La. 696, 181 So. 2d 397 (1966).

[217] *Thibodeaux v. Bordelon*, 740 F.2d 329, 336 (5th Cir. 1984).

[218] *Marchant v. Pennsylvania R. Co.*, 153 U.S. 380, 390 (1894).

This implies that all courts of the same level within a state should operate similar to one another to safeguard due process. Likewise, some pundits have even advocated that "freedom from arbitrary adjudicative procedures" should be recognized as a substantive element of liberty.[219] Yet, despite this jurisprudence mayor's courts continue to operate without procedural rules or by inconsistent rules, and as a result due process guarantees are jeopardized.

One potential risk is created by the fact that mayor's courts are not mandated to follow any formal rules for discovery. This is because the rules for civil discovery are provided in the Code of Civil Procedure art. 1420 *et seq.*, and the rules for criminal discovery are provided in the Code of Criminal Procedure art. 716 *et seq.* Neither of which governs mayor's courts. As the Supreme Court stated, "[t]he discovery provisions ... and procedural articles affecting right to trial were established to ensure due process."[220] Without the codes of procedure there exists the possibility that mayors will forbid defendants from being allowed to both inspect or object to evidence that will be used against him ahead of trial. By depriving this ability a defendant might not be able to reasonably prepare a good defense or argument for the case against him. Even if a defendant were allowed to inspect evidence ahead of time, there wouldn't be anything to limit a mayor from arbitrarily calling in a surprise witnesses or evidence at the last minute before trial.

Furthermore, if mayors were allowed to proceed under the "spirit" of the codes (as mentioned in La. Code Crim. Proc. art. 3), the opportunity exists for mayors to arbitrarily pick and choose provisions from both codes of procedure, and use them collectively in a way that was not intended by the legislature. Other than the minimal constitutional boundaries, there is nothing stopping a mayor in a criminal case from unilaterally employing the liberal civil discovery provisions to broaden the more limited scope of discovery in criminal

---

[219] William Van Alstynet, *"The New Property": Adjudicative Due Process in the Administrative State*, 62 Cornell L. Rev. 445, 487 (1977).
[220] *State, Dep't of Transp. & Dev. v. Stumpf*, 458 So. 2d 448, 451-52 (La. 1984).

cases (or even supplementing with his made up rules) while the defendant is denied the same opportunity.[221]

If the mayor acting as prosecutor is able to circumvent the discovery rules, this could potentially violate a defendant's right against self incrimination, or right to a fair trial.[222] This is because under the civil code of procedure a party can be compelled to testify, or turn over evidence that would be excluded under criminal procedure rules.[223] Being that the Fifth Amendment right against self incrimination needs to be plead or it is waived, and the Sixth Amendment can also be waived, most defendants with little legal training could fail to realize this and end up being convicted based on their own testimony. Furthermore, civil evidence could give the mayor as prosecutor a lead in criminal cases or a "link in the chain" to other evidence, which might normally be protected under the criminal code of procedure.

To make matters worse, any evidence that is produced is not subject to the Louisiana Code of Evidence. This is because the underlying principles of the Code of Evidence only serve as "guides" to the admissibility of evidence in all proceedings before mayor's

---

[221] The Code of Civil Procedure requires liberal discovery, as it requires full disclose before trial "regarding any matter, not privileged, which is relevant to the subject matter involved in the pending action... [that] appears reasonably calculated to lead to the discovery of admissible evidence." La. Code Civ. Proc. art. 1422. Civil discovery seeks to make all parties fully inform prior to trial so as to avoid wasteful litigation in court.

Conversely, the Code of Criminal Procedure's intended purpose is to provide for justice. *See* La. Code Crim. Proc. art. 2. The discovery articles in the criminal code of procedure are not as liberal, as most provisions require that a motion to the court be made to obtain permission to seek discovery from the other party.

[222] An argument could also be made that expanding discovery in criminal cases decreases the integrity of the criminal justice system, which deprives defendants of due process. As a public policy matter, to protect the criminal justice system rules of procedure should be implemented in the mayor's courts.

[223] La. Code Civ. Proc. art. 222.1.

courts.[224] Since the mayor acts as both the prosecutor and adjudicator, he can essentially present and admit any evidence that he wants at his discretion. Without the rules of evidence there is nothing to safeguard evidence (other than minimum constitutional requirements) from being admitted that would otherwise be inadmissible under the Code of Evidence. For example, one study of mayor's courts reported that in small towns most mayors are usually very familiar with the affairs and problems of their citizens, and during court proceedings have brought up unrelated outside knowledge about defendants.[225] Moreover, many defendants might feel reluctant to object to evidence that the mayor presents out of fear of retaliation for objecting to the mayor. Likewise, some people might overlook any unwarranted evidence by the mayor because of the policy assumption that all judges are fair and neutral, and would never try to use their position to sneak in prohibited evidence.

An additional risk created by not having to comply with any code of procedure is the potential for receiving inadequate notice when criminal charges are initiated. The procedures for providing notice to a defendant when to appear in court for both civil and criminal proceedings are provided in the civil and criminal codes respectively.[226] As a result, mayor's courts may determine when and how they want to issue service of process, with the only be limit being the indistinct constitutional requirement of reasonableness. For example, one study of mayor's courts in Louisiana reported that notification of when to appear is usually issued by mail, and rarely

---

[224] La. Code Evid. Ann. art. 1101B. states "[e]xcept as otherwise provided by Article 1101(A)(2) and other legislation, in the following proceedings, the principles underlying this Code shall serve as guides to the admissibility of evidence. The specific exclusionary rules and other provisions, however, shall be applied only to the extent that they tend to promote the purposes of the proceeding.... (5) All proceedings before mayors' courts and justice of the peace courts."

[225] David A. Alvarez & Walter W Troxey, *Louisiana Mayor's Court Procedures: Recommendations and Observations* 11 (1971).

[226] *See* La. Code Crim. Proc. Title XXV Compulsory Process; La. Code Civ. Proc. Title II Citation and Service of Process.

served.[227] Obviously under either code of procedure service would have to have been made by a law enforcement officer or authorized another person.

Similarly, Under La. Code Crim. Proc. art. 382 the method for instituting a criminal prosecution for violation of an ordinance shall be by affidavit or information with supporting affidavit. However, since the Code of Criminal Procedure is not applicable to mayor's courts, due process only requires that a defendant be afforded reasonable notice of the charges against him.[228] The question of what constitutes reasonable notice is something that the Code of Criminal Procedure sought to answer, however, without the code the question of reasonable is anyone's guess. Note that the official comments under La. Code Crim. Proc. art. 382 mention that while great informality will prevail in mayor's court cases, prosecutions should be instituted by affidavit in order to meet the minimal requirements for instituting a prosecution.[229] However, one court has held that an affidavit is not necessary. Rather, that court held that ample notice of the charges against a defendant was given when documents setting forth specific facts were attached to a generic bill of information.[230] However, the court did not mention any details about what minimum level or type of notice would be sufficient.

C. PROSPECTIVE SOLUTIONS

A proponent of mayor's courts could argue that these courts in Louisiana operate within constitutional limits because it's okay to have less due process protections for hearings with lessor punishments. This is because due process is flexible, and not every

---

[227] David A. Alvarez & Walter W Troxey, *Louisiana Mayor's Court Procedures: Recommendations and Observations* 12 (1971).

[228] *City of Kenner v. Marquis*, 98-418 (La. App. 5 Cir. 6/4/98), 715 So. 2d 85, 88-89 *writ denied,* 98-1806 (La. 10/16/98), 726 So. 2d 907

[229] *See also* La. Att'y Gen. Op. No. 1978-326.

[230] *City of Kenner v. Marquis*, 98-418 (La. App. 5 Cir. 6/4/98), 715 So. 2d 85, 90 *writ denied,* 98-1806 (La. 10/16/98), 726 So. 2d 907

type of hearing requires the same amount of protection. Additionally, an argument could be made that less protection is needed because mayors preside over court all the time and have been doing so since before Louisiana was a state. However, these arguments would fail because the current scheme that mayor's courts operate under provides virtually no due process protection. Furthermore, there is no way to tell how defendants are being sentenced for convictions because there is no reporting system.

The only solution that would safeguard against both constitutional problems presented would be to abolish the mayor's courts completely and replace them with or have their cases handled by a city court, parish, or district court. Since mayor's courts are empowered by the constitution the only way for this to be accomplished would be by a constitutional amendment. That would require an initiative be placed on the ballot, which receives a majority of votes by the people.

Alternatively, measures can be taken that would help safeguard each problem separately. This section discusses a few prospective solutions that would help protect due process for each problem separately. First, this section will provide some solutions for the problem of the bias mayor. Secondly, this section will detail some possible solutions to assist with the problem created by the lack of formal procedural rules.

1. PROSPECTIVE SOLUTIONS FOR THE MAYOR BIAS PROBLEM

This section proposes three solutions to help safeguard against biased mayors casting predetermined judgments. The first solution is to mandate some form of reporting requirement to keep track of the number of cases and convictions processed through mayor's courts. The second prospective solution is to enact legislation requiring that only a licensed attorney can preside over mayor's courts. A third solution would be to make applicable the Code of Judicial Conduct to mayors or their appointed magistrates presiding over mayor's courts

The first prospective solutions to the mayor bias problem involve additional oversight of mayor's court. This includes instituting a reporting requirement, similar to those already in place for city courts, district courts, appeals courts, and the Supreme Court.[231] Mayor's courts should be required to report to the Louisiana Supreme Court additional data than just the amount of fines collected in a year. Currently, the Supreme Court doesn't require mayor's courts to report specific conviction data to them as with other courts. An example that illustrates this fact is seen in the 2013 Annual Report of the Judicial Council of the Supreme Court how the Court Management Information Systems (CMIS) office only received data on traffic cases from 5 mayor's courts for that year.[232] Moreover, the only *quasi* reporting that mayor's courts are required to do is tied into payments they must make to support the development of a statewide court case database. They're required pay the Supreme Court $1 dollar for every conviction if their population is less than 2,000 and $3 dollars for every conviction if their population is more than 2,000.[233]

A second proposed solution would be for the legislature to mandate that a licensed attorney either be appointed as the magistrate for every mayor's court, or elected as every other judge in the state. This would thereby help eliminate the opportunity for mayors to exhibit any bias in adjudicate cases, and thus help safeguard that a defendant in mayor's court would have a fair and impartial arbiter. Granted the potential for some bias may still be present since the

---

[231] Mayor's courts are not included in the list of "courts of limited jurisdiction" that are required to have any changes to the amount of court costs first reviewed by the Judicial Council of the Supreme Court of Louisiana. La. Rev. Stat. § 13:62. Additionally, the Judicial Council of the Supreme Court of Louisiana is expressly prohibited from adopting determinate standards and guidelines for determining whether new judgeships should be created in mayor's courts as part of its report to the legislature. *See* La. Rev. Stat. § 13:61; *See* House Concurrent Resolution No. 143 of the 2011 Regular Legislative Session.

[232] Supreme Court of Louisiana, Annual Report 2013 of the Judicial Council of the Supreme Court 9 (2013).

[233] La. Code Crim. Proc. art. 887.F(1) Court cost for implementation of the master plan for the development of a trial court case management information system.

appointed attorney can still be terminated by the mayor. However, this method would still reduce the risk because the appointed attorney would not have an executive duty like the mayor to raise revenues for the city, which would provide some level of remoteness from possible financial temptations. Also, other protections such as the Rules of Profession Conduct would then to come into play as the appointed magistrate must by law be an attorney, who would have to comply with these rules.[234] Moreover, this solution would also allow for each political entity to maintain some level of autonomy over municipal violations, however, for mayors to continue presiding over court they would need to be a lawyer.

A third proposed solution would be for the Louisiana Supreme Court to amend the Code of Judicial Conduct to make it clearly applicable to mayors or their appointed magistrates presiding over mayor's courts. This is because the Code of Judicial Conduct provides more protection than due process requires. For example, Cannon 2 mandates that judges "shall avoid impropriety and the appearance of impropriety in all activities."[235]

Whether the Code of Judicial Conduct currently applies to mayors is a grey area subject to interpretation, and needs to be clarified by the Supreme Court. At the outset it should be noted that as a government official the Code of Governmental Ethics would require a mayor to act impartially for the proper operation of democratic government.[236] However, the Code of Governmental Ethics states that "[a]ll judges, as defined by the Code of Judicial Conduct, shall be governed exclusively by the provisions of the Code of Judicial Conduct, which shall be administered by the Judiciary Commission."[237] Yet the Code of Judicial Conduct states that it is only applicable to "[a]ll elected judges and anyone, whether or not a lawyer, who is an officer of a *court of record* performing judicial functions... is a judge for the

---

[234] Note that non-attorney mayors are not subject to the Rules of Professional Conduct.

[235] *Caperton*, 556 U.S. at 890; LA ST CJC Canon 2.

[236] La. Rev. Stat. § 42:1101.

[237] La. Rev. Stat. § 42:1167.

purpose of this Code... All judges shall comply with this Code."[238] (Emphasis added). As stated above mayor's courts are not courts of record, therefore, mayors and appointed magistrates are not included in the definition of judge under the Code, and do not have to comply with it.[239]

To make the matter more confusing, the Attorney General's Office has issued the opinion that mayor's courts and its magistrates are subject to the Code of Judicial Conduct by virtue of their being part of the judiciary under the constitution.[240] Furthermore, Rule XXIII of the Louisiana Supreme Court, expressly includes "a mayor who performs judicial functions" in the definition of judge for the purpose of proceedings before the judiciary commission.[241] Rule XXIII further proscribes a special discipline is applicable to mayors, which includes "censure or suspension with salary from the performance of judicial functions."[242]

So while it seems as though the Judiciary Commission would have jurisdiction over mayors in their judicial capacity, the Commission has yet to establish any rules governing them. Vague definitions such as this further contribute to the issue of fairness, as most mayors likely will find it difficult to determine what rules apply to them if any. Therefore, in the interest of fairness the Judicial Code of Conduct should she amended to clearly include mayors functioning in a judicial capacity.

While anyone of these three prospective solutions would help safeguard against an unfair trial, I cannot recommend one solution over another in preference. In fact, all three of these solutions should be incorporated for the best result. Nevertheless, even if all three recommendations were implemented, they would likely only help

---

[238] LA ST CJC Compliance (Compliance with the Code of Judicial Conduct).

[239] *Sledge*, 324 So. 2d at 358.

[240] *See* La. Const. art. V, § 5(A); See La. Const. art. V, § 20.

[241] La. Sup. Ct. R. XXIII, § 2(b).

[242] *See* La. Sup. Ct. R. XXIII, § 2(e) ("with respect to a mayor who performs judicial functions, 'discipline' means censure or suspension with salary from the performance of judicial functions").

reduce the risk although the potential for bias may still exists. This is because as long as a mayor has the duty to raise revenue for his city in his executive capacity, there will always be the potential for the mayor render predetermined judgments that result in an increase in general fund revenue. It will be very difficult if not impossible for a mayor to separate himself from this duty, and therefore every possible step that can be taken to reduce the risk of an unfair trial should be taken.

2. PROPOSED SOLUTIONS TO HELP SAFEGUARD AGAINST THE LACK OF FORMAL PROCEDURAL RULES

To comply with the requirements of procedural due process one of the following three proposed safeguards should be implemented to reduce the risk of erroneous deprivation of liberty and property. Three proposed solutions to this problem would be (1) to amend the language of both codes of procedure to make them applicable to mayor's courts, (2) enact a uniform set of rules specifically for mayor's courts, or (3) implement a plan where each court would be mandated to adopt one or both of the Louisiana codes of procedure, or enact their own sets of procedural rules.

The first proposed solution would be to legislatively amend the language of both the civil and criminal codes of procedure to be applicable to mayor's courts. Of these three proposed safeguards, this one would establish the most uniform system of procedure across the state, but it would also be the most onerous on the mayor's courts. In order for both codes of procedure to be applicable, significant changes in the operational aspects would need to be made by each court to be able to comply with the mandates of the codes. Essentially, mayor's courts would need to adapt and function similarly to the way other courts of limited jurisdiction do.

The second proposed solution would be for the legislature to enact a new uniform set of rules and procedure that would govern all mayor's courts around the state uniformly. This method would not be as onerous to the mayor's courts, yet some minor changes would likely still need to me made from the current functions of each court. This method would create a uniform system of procedure for mayor's courts across the state, while at the same time maintain some of the informal aspects that the legislature intended when allowing for these courts.

The third proposed solution would call for a mandate that each individual mayor's court either adopt one or both of the current codes of procedure, or alternatively enact their own a set of procedural rules. Municipalities choosing to enact their own procedural rules would do so in a way similar to the mandates governing administrative agencies in Administrative Procedure Act.[243] Under this method each municipality would then have to file a copy their enacted rules with the Supreme Court or applicable state office, so that its rules of procedure would be easily accessible to the public to inspect. Although under this proposal each mayor's court could have different procedural rules, the risk of erroneous deprivation is still reduced. Reason being that each court will at least be governed under some form of rules for procedure. The key to this is having the rules easily accessible to the public and in a central location so that it will be reasonably clear to defendants how their trial will be conducted. Additionally, this scheme will provide the greatest opportunity for each court to maintain a level of informality specific to their geographical needs, while providing a minimal safeguard from a procedural standpoint.

Out of these three proposed solutions I would recommend the first solution, which is that both the codes of criminal and civil procedure be amended to incorporate mayor's courts. If the constitution is going to continue authorizing the existence of these courts, then every

---

[243] La. Rev. Stat. § 49:952. Note that mayor's courts are judicially created under the Constitution and therefore may not be governed under the Administrative Procedure Act. Additionally, La. Rev. Stat. § 49:951(2) excludes from the definition of "agency" the following: "the legislature or any branch, committee, or officer thereof, any political subdivision, as defined in La. Const. art. VI, § 44, and any board, commission, department, agency, officer, or other entity thereof, and the courts."

reasonable step should be taken to protect the rights of the accused. This is especially true since the possibility of jail time or probation is an optional penalty for some offenses. Not to mention some traffic offense convictions could have other repercussions such as increases in auto insurance premiums, or license suspensions for certain commercial driver's license holders in some situations. Additionally, it is not unreasonable to hold mayor's courts to the same standards as other courts of limited jurisdiction, which prosecute similar type offenses such as traffic tickets and misdemeanor offenses. Granted, a relaxed or informal procedural atmosphere may be desired to help move cases along more conveniently, but that option should be left solely up to the accused whether to waive formal procedure and not to a potentially biased mayor.

CONCLUSION

Mayor's courts are tribunals vested under the constitution, which have jurisdiction to try violations of municipal ordinances. The mayor or appointed magistrate presides over the court, and may impose fines and imprisonment for breaches of ordinances. In establishing these courts, the legislature intended for the proceedings to be informal, including allowing for non-lawyer mayors to preside over court without any formal rules of procedure. However, mayors inherently have potential temptations that will cause them to be biased against the accused being tried. As a result there exists a danger of depriving defendants of their procedural due process guarantees. Additional safeguards should be instituted to comport with the Fourteenth Amendment. As part of the solution, some form of procedural rules should be implemented to govern these courts. Because by not doing anything these courts will continue to operate outside of established safeguards, which will always make it reasonable to question whether a defendant received a fair trial.

APPENDIX

TABLE 1: Fines collected during the 2013 fiscal year

Municipality	Fines as % of General Fund	Fines Revenue	Total General Fund Revenue	Police Chief	Pop.
Georgetown	94.47%	$639,634	$677,104	Elected	327
Fenton	89.36%	$737,022	$824,749	Elected	379
Dodson	88.64%	$411,522	$464,266	Elected	337
Washington (NL)	83.67%	$1,313,139	$1,569,505	Elected	964
Henderson	83.05%	$705,383	$849,298	Elected	1,674
Baskin	78.04%	$285,146	$365,404	Elected	254
Robeline	77.47%	$276,725	$357,186	Elected	174
Pioneer	71.65%	$69,292	$96,704	Unclear	156
Fisher	69.18%	$133,208	$192,548	Elected	230
Clarence	67.64%	$160,791	$237,708	Elected	499
Reeves	66.20%	$384,644	$581,055	Elected	232
Port Vincent	65.77%	$182,218	$277,051	Appointed	741
Creola	65.53%	$158,664	$242,110	Elected	213
Pollock	63.82%	$276,258	$432,894	Elected	469
Tullos	62.80%	$121,569	$193,584	Elected	385
Cotton Valley	60.97%	$144,714	$237,335	Elected	1,009
Merryville	57.35%	$151,719	$264,550	Elected	1,103
Tickfaw	55.68%	$366,905	$659,007	Elected	694
Port Barre	52.76%	$679,373	$1,287,644	Elected	2,055
Dry Prong	51.47%	$72,138	$140,162	Appointed	436
Rosepine	51.10%	$183,402	$358,905	Elected	1,692
Gilbert	51.09%	$101,556	$198,784	Elected	521
French Settlement	50.29%	$135,425	$269,291	Elected	1,116
Maurice	48.68%	$221,460	$454,927	Elected	964
Vinton	47.77%	$776,731	$1,626,090	Elected	3,212
McNary	46.70%	$74,516	$159,573	Appointed	211

Municipality	Fines as % of General Fund	Fines Revenue	Total General Fund Revenue	Police Chief	Pop.
Woodworth	45.90%	$936,494	$2,040,359	Appointed	1,096
Livonia	45.63%	$518,432	$1,136,243	Elected	1,442
North Hodge	44.91%	$78,285	$174,322	Elected	388
Anacoco	44.63%	$104,503	$234,176	Elected	869
Saline	44.44%	$20,911	$47,057	Elected	277
Delta	44.20%	$77,570	$175,484	Unclear	284
New Llano	43.24%	$528,258	$1,221,588	Elected	2,504
Turkey Creek	42.05%	$73,248	$174,186	Elected	441
Grand Coteau	40.42%	$335,842	$830,923	Elected	947
Pine Prairie	39.37%	$211,152	$536,281	Elected	1,610
Forest Hill	38.22%	$202,907	$530,832	Elected	818
Norwood	38.17%	$35,828	$93,864	Appointed	322
Kinder	37.41%	$361,612	$966,713	Elected	2,477
Sibley	37.07%	$83,140	$224,289	Elected	1,218
DeQuincy (NL)*	36.74%	$238,813	$650,033	Appointed	3,235
Bonita	35.94%	$51,502	$143,287	Appointed	284
Kilbourne	35.44%	$17,083	$48,197	Elected	416
Mangham	33.89%	$92,009	$271,456	Elected	672
Ashland	33.03%	$6,933	$20,992	Elected	269
Clinton (NL)+	31.79%	$279,887	$880,428	Appointed	1,653
Bernice	30.82%	$89,827	$291,454	Elected	1689
Wilson	30.72%	$43,065	$140,207	Appointed	595
Pearl River**	29.97%	$208,224	$694,835	Elected	2,506
Gretna	29.43%	$5,307,249	$18,031,475	Elected	17,736
Waterproof	28.26%	$171,910	$608,361	Appointed	688
Iowa	28.09%	$412,817	$1,469,694	Elected	2,996
Oil City	28.06%	$94,919	$338,310	Appointed	1,008
Olla	26.54%	$281,280	$1,059,640	Elected	1,385
Oberlin	26.53%	$135,767	$511,842	Elected	1,770
Grayson	26.09%	$55,467	$212,587	Elected	532
Sterlington	25.98%	$224,752	$865,039	Elected	1,594
Golden Meadow	25.65%	$598,663	$2,333,517	Elected	2,101
Morse	25.35%	$29,852	$117,753	Elected	812
Cheneyville	25.35%	$105,912	$417,815	Appointed	625
Krotz Springs	24.56%	$197,078	$802,571	Elected	1,198
Lake Providence	24.38%	$305,097	$1,251,425	Elected	3,991

Municipality	Fines as % of General Fund	Fines Revenue	Total General Fund Revenue	Police Chief	Pop.
Hessmer	23.09%	$68,972	$298,758	Elected	802
Varnado	22.63%	$18,616	$82,279	Elected	1,461
Elton	22.38%	$52,179	$233,119	Elected	1128
Sun++	21.77%	$35,598	$163,530	Appointed	470
Ida	21.72%	$19,673	$90,556	Elected	221
Cankton	21.59%	$23,908	$110,717	Unclear	484
Glenmora	21.16%	$171,101	$808,491	Elected	1,342
Killian	20.83%	$58,136	$279,090	Appointed	1,206
Urania	20.50%	$46,732	$227,981	Elected	1,313
Rodessa	20.47%	$9,281	$45,347	Appointed	270
Dubach	20.40%	$65,393	$320,610	Elected	961
Slaughter	20.19%	$99,898	$494,895	Elected	997
Estherwood	20.14%	$31,683	$157,336	Elected	889
Sunset	20.13%	$123,183	$612,048	Elected	2,897
Heflin	20.03%	$9,350	$46,679	Elected	247
Moreauville	18.73%	$39,984	$213,468	Appointed	929
Lecompte	17.91%	$103,806	$579,502	Appointed	1,227
Delhi	17.73%	$245,588	$1,384,838	Elected	2,919
Florien	17.47%	$190,551	$1,090,729	Elected	633
Stonewall	17.42%	$157,069	$901,748	Elected	1,814
Ferriday	17.39%	$512,499	$2,947,419	Appointed	3,511
Walker	17.16%	$729,980	$4,254,323	Elected	6138
Greenwood	16.54%	$265,274	$1,603,659	Appointed	3,219
Hornbeck	16.33%	$19,077	$116,797	Elected	480
Ball	16.32%	$295,702	$1,811,593	Elected	4,000
Westwego	15.79%	$1,997,967	$12,650,506	Elected	8,534
Pleasant Hill	15.43%	$26,018	$168,629	Elected	723
Brusly	15.32%	$311,467	$2,033,548	Elected	2,589
Welsh	15.20%	$233,898	$1,539,088	Elected	3,226
Grambling	14.89%	$286,277	$1,922,829	Appointed	4,949
Harahan	14.16%	$648,240	$4,578,350	Elected	9,277
Lockport	13.93%	$118,434	$850,089	Elected	2,578
Livingston	12.54%	$201,731	$1,608,695	Elected	1,769
Dubberly	12.11%	$3,075	$25,393	Elected	273
Richwood++	11.99%	$136,023	$1,134,743	Appointed	3,392
Campti	11.89%	$26,079	$219,272	Elected	1056

Municipality	Fines as % of General Fund	Fines Revenue	Total General Fund Revenue	Police Chief	Pop.
Abita Springs	11.56%	$120,423	$1,041,839	Appointed	2,365
Sicily Island	10.57%	$15,302	$144,704	Appointed	526

(NL) Non-Lawrason Act charter municipality

*   In DeQuincy fines are distributed into a public safety special revenue fund, and not into the general fund.

**   In Pearl River fines are distributed between the general fund and a police special revenue fund.

+   Data gathered from the 2012 Legislative Auditor Report.

++   Data gathered from the 2011 Legislative Auditor Report.

Source:

Table represents data gathered from the latest available Louisiana Legislative Auditor reports as of 12/13/ 2014. Note that legislative auditor reports only report fine and forfeiture amounts collected by the municipality, and do not specify whether funds derived from the mayor's court; the Louisiana Secretary of State elected officials database, available at http://www.sos. la.gov/ElectionsAndVoting/FindPublicOfficials/Pages/ElectedOfficialsSearch.aspx; and the Louisiana Municipal Association directory, available at http://www.lma.org/LMA20/About/ Municipal_Directory/LMA20/Municipalities/Municipality_Directory.aspx?hkey=7d04be94-a2e5-4d5d-b20a-aeebefb77e4e.

Municipal populations represent figures from the 2010 U.S. census.

ABOUT THE AUTHOR

Floyd A. Buras, III is a practicing attorney in the New Orleans, Louisiana metro area. He graduated *Magna Cum Laude* from Loyola University New Orleans, College of Law, where he earned his Juris Doctorate, and is a William L. Crowe, Sr. scholar. He also has a Bachelor of Arts in Political Science from the University of Minnesota.

The Author wishes to express special thanks to his family for their support during his research, and also to Professor Andrea Armstrong, Esq. for her insightful feedback.

THIS BOOK SHOULD NOT BE INTERPRETED AS LEGAL ADVICE

The information provided in this book is intended for general information and scholarly purposes only, and should not be relied upon in lieu of consultation with appropriate legal advisors in your own jurisdiction. The content of this book may not be accurate due to the fact that the law is constantly changing and may differ by jurisdiction. The Author makes no warranties or guarantees that the information is accurate, complete, or up-to-date.